AF651822

Socio-Linguistic Situation in North-East India

About the Author

Pauthang Haokip obtained his degrees of M.A. and Ph.D. in Linguistics from North Eastern Hills University, Shillong. Thereafter he joined the Department of Linguistics, Assam University, Silchar as Assistant Professor. His research areas include Phonetics and Phonology, Tibeto-Burman Linguistic and Socio-linguistics. He has been actively associated with Central Institute of Indian Languages, Mysore thereby completing a major project entitled "The Comparative Study of *Kuki-Chin* Language Spoken in Manipur".

Socio-Linguistic Situation in North-East India

Pauthang Haokip

CONCEPT PUBLISHING COMPANY PVT. LTD.
NEW DELHI-110059

© Pauthang Haokip

All rights reserved. No part of this work may be reproduced, stored, adapted, or transmitted in any form or by any means, electronic, mechanical, photocopying, micro-filming recording or otherwise, or translated in any language, without the prior written permission of the copyright owner and the publisher. The book is sold subject to the condition that it shall not, by way of trade or otherwise, be lent, resold, hired out, or otherwise circulated without the prior publisher's written consent in any form of binding or cover other than that in which it is published.

The views and opinions expressed in this book are author(s) own and the facts reported by him have been verified to the extent possible, and the publishers are not in anyway liable for the same.

ISBN-13: 978-81-8069-760-9

First Published 2011

Published and Printed by

Concept
Since 1974

Concept Publishing Company Pvt. Ltd.
Regd. Office:
A/15-16, Commercial Block, Mohan Garden
New Delhi-110059 (India)
Phones : 25351460, 25351794, *Fax* : 091-11-25357109
Email : publishing@conceptpub.com
Website: www.conceptpub.com

Editorial Office:
H-13, Bali Nagar, New Delhi-110 015, India.

Cataloging in Publication Data--*Courtesy:* D.K. Agencies (P) Ltd. <docinfo@dkagencies.com>

Haokip, Pauthang.
Socio-linguistic situation in North-east India / Pauthang Haokip.
p. cm.
Includes bibliographical references (p.) and index.
ISBN 9788180697609

1. Sociolinguistics--India, Northeastern. 2. Sociolinguistics--India--Manipur. I. Title.

DDC 306.4409541 22

Foreword

Since "Linguistic Survey of India (1903)" a lot of changes had taken place with respect to language situation in the country, especially in North-Eastern region of India. However, till today, no linguist has seriously dealt with the present socio-linguistic situation of this sector. The main reason is that such a survey project requires large man-power and financial support.

I am not questioning the academic proficiency of the data collectors and their supervisors in the Survey Report, but these data were collected more than a century ago. Considering the geographical and political inaccessibility in most parts of North-East India during the period of data collection, one must agree that it was humanly impossible for the researchers to gather all the details of data they intended to gather, and analyze them. Despite all the difficulties the data were professionally collected and analyzed in the last survey report.

Due to lack of current information, the linguists had to rely only on the information supplied in the Survey Report although a number of changes had taken place and numerous discoveries were made during this intervening period of more than a century. Sadly enough, we have no other option even now for whoever publishes a research article or a book pertaining to language and linguistic situation in North East India has to rely on the Linguistic Survey of India (1903) since this is the sole reference book available with us even to this day. Hence, with regard to the pertaining situation, the Central Institute of Indian Languages, Mysore, initiated a proposal to launch *New Linguistic Survey of India* about a decade ago, but this could not be implemented effectively due to various reasons.

Having gone through the manuscript of the present book "Socio-Linguistic Situation in North East India", I am so impressed to realize that the author had taken pain on his own effort to collect rich and comprehensive data urgently needed for up-to-date information about the language and the linguistic situation in North-East India, particularly in the State of Manipur.

The book will be helpful for all those who intend to venture into the field of socio-linguistic studies in general, and the linguistic situation in North-East India, in particular. I wish the author the best of success.

Dr. Kedutso Kapfo,
Associate Professor,
Central Institute of Indian Languages,
Ministry of Human Resource Development, Govt. of India,
Manasagangotri, Mysore-570 006.

Preface

North-East India has always been a fascinating field of socio-linguistic investigations. The different states of North-East India have been in the limelight of newspapers and national news for social unrests which erupted from time to time among the various ethnic groups. Sometimes, such ethnic tensions are often directed on linguistic basis. Thus, the present book entitled **"Socio-Linguistic Situation in North-East India"** is an attempt in this direction towards describing the relationship among the various linguistic groups in North-East India in general and Manipur in particular which constitutes a major portion of this book. The nature of social organizations of different linguistic groups in the North-East India is often so complex that at times it overrides linguistic criterion for the determination of language and language groupings. The social relationships through which different linguistic groups enter with one another are often political in nature and are seldom based on genetic relationship. Thus, North-East India presents an intriguing field of research in that, a researcher can land up making wrong conclusions about the relationship of the various linguistic groups of the region unless one thoroughly understands which groups of languages are genetically related and distinct from other social or political groupings. It is on account of lack of proper understanding about the genetic relationship of different linguistic groups that, a dozen of Kuki-Chin languages (Old Kukis) have been wrongly understood to be Nagas with whom they share no linguistic affinity.

To dispel the often misunderstood concept among the Northeasterners that language boundary corresponds to tribe boundary, the volume discusses two separate cases of the Kuki-Chin dialects which are mutually intelligible and different speech forms of Tangkhul which are conceived to be mutually unintelligible as evidence to show that language boundary may not always correspond to tribe boundary.

Another important phenomenon which will be of great interest and concern for the language activists is that the lesser known languages of Manipur are in the process of great endangerment owing to the pressure from cross-sections of the dominant ethnic communities who are pressing hard for greater ethnic recognition from the government, both state and central.

The present volume, while highlighting the socio-linguistic situation of Manipur also raises the issue of mother tongue education in the state and suggests remedial measures which if followed will be appropriate for a pluralistic society like Manipur.

It is hoped that the present volume will be found useful and meaningful to socio-linguists, linguists, typologists and other social scientists working on the languages/tribes of the region for full understanding of the often confused relationship which holds the various ethnic communities of the region together.

The author wholeheartedly invites suggestions and criticisms for the improvement of the present volume.

Pauthang Haokip

Acknowledgements

It is a pleasure to place on record my sense of gratitude to the following persons for helping me in some way or the other during the entire preparation of this book.

1. To Professor S.S. Bhattarcharya, Former Senior Research Officer (Language) & Head, Language Division Office of the Registrar General, India, Kolkata for his insightful comments and suggestions on the languages of North East India.
2. To Professor Rajesh Sachdeva, Director In-Charge, CIIL, Mysore who not only encouraged me but also helped me chisel out some rough edges by his perspective comments on the preliminary analysis.
3. To Professor Yashawant Singh with whom I discussed the overall linguistic situation of Manipur.
4. To Dr. Kedutsa Kapfo who himself has taken personal interest in going through my manuscript and arranging all technical helps in the publication of my book.
5. Lastly, I would like to thank Concept Publishing Company Pvt. Ltd. and Mr. Ashok Kumar Mittal for taking initiative to publish this book.

Pauthang Haokip

Contents

List of Tables and Figures

TABLES

FIGURES

Organisation of the Book

The book is organised as follows:

Chapter 1 introduces the languages of North-East India and discusses the problem of classifying the languages of the North-East owing to socio-political factors which overrides linguistic criterion in determining language (s) spoken in the region.

Chapter 2 explores the typological sketch of the Tibeto-Burman of languages of the North-East.

Chapter 3 discusses the position of Kuki-Chin-Naga within the Tibeto-Burman family by exploring the defects of the major classifications.

Chapter 4 deals with the linguistic situation of Manipur with special reference to the Old Kuki languages who have declared themselves to be Nagas with whom they share no linguistic affinity. The chapter also discusses at length the minorities and endangered languages of Manipur as well as the problems of mother tongue education for tribal languages in Manipur.

Chapter 5 discusses the linguistic situation of Kuki-Chin in Manipur.

Chapter 6 is devoted to introducing the Kuki-Chin people.

Lastly, an appendix showing the comparative vocabulary of six selected Kuki-Chin languages has been provided to show how far these languages are similar or different from each other. Second appendix shows word correspondences among the Kuki-Chin languages.

1

North East India

1.0. INTRODUCTION

Located in the North-Eastern most part of India, North-East shares 4,500 km long international border with five neighbouring countries—Bangladesh, Bhutan, Myanmar, China, and Nepal. The whole of North-East region is connected to the rest of the country just by a strait of 22 km land corridor through Siliguri in the state of West Bengal—a link that is often referred to as "Chicken's Neck". The North-Eastern states are bounded by the mountainous region of the Himalayas in its eastern slopes with Arunachal Pradesh rising all the way up to its border with Tibet. Linguistically, North-East India is the most heterogeneous area which houses almost half of the languages listed by the Census of India. North-East is surrounded by various subgroups speaking the Tibeto-Burman languages—from Arunachal Pradesh on the north to Nagaland, Manipur and Mizoram in the east. In addition to the major linguistic groups in the North-East India, viz., Tibeto-Burman, Indo-Aryan and Austro-Asiatic, there are some languages and lingua francas used in inter-lingual contact situations which are not even documented. The socio-linguistic profile of the eight states in the region offers a wide variety of speech forms and intriguing typology of pluralistic situations.

Assam

Located just below the Eastern Himalayan foothills, Assam is surrounded by other North-Eastern states and occupies an important place in the region. It forms a gateway to the rest of the region. It is also the largest in size and population and lie at the centre of Brahmaputra valley. The state of Assam is somewhat different geographically, ethnically and linguistically from the six hill states. Assamese an Indo-Aryan language is the major language of the state as well as the lingua franca for many ethnic communities in the state. Apart from Assamese, Sylheti (a variety of Bengali) is widely spoken throughout the Cachar district and Barak valley of lower Assam. Apart from Assamese and Bengali, Rajbongshi or Deshibhasa and Bishnupriya are other Indo-Aryan languages spoken in the state of Assam. Rajbongshi is spoken in the western part of Assam and in entire North Bengal and has a higher influence of Bodo group of the Tibeto-Burman family. Bishnupriya is spoken in Cachar, Hailakandi and Karimganj districts of Barak Valley. It is also spoken in parts of Manipur, North Tripura and in Bangladesh. Over years of contact with Manipuri, it has incorporated a lot of Manipuri lexical items. According to Masica (1991), Bishnupriya retains a pre-Bengali features and is closer to Bengali and Assamese. According to Census of India 2001, Bishnupriya is spoken by 77,545 speakers. The total number of speakers statewise are: Manipur = 1,457, Tripura = 21,716 and Assam = 53,812. Apart from these Indo-Aryan languages, there are substantial numbers of Bodo-Garo and Kuki-Naga subgroups of the Tibeto-Burman family spoken in different parts of Assam. The Bodo-Garo subgroup is not only spoken in the hills surrounding it, but, also along the low laying plains of Brahmaputra. These include Bodo, Dimasa, Rabha, and various Koch dialects (or languages) in lower (western) part of the valley, and Deuri, which is spoken by a small group in the upper valley. Tiwa (formerly known as Lulung) is spoken primarily in Karbi Anglong District of Assam. The Kuki-Naga languages are primarily spoken in autonomous District council of N.C. Hills and in the surrounding hills of Cachar District. These include Rongmei, Zeme, Hmar, Bete, and Thadou-Kuki, etc. It should be noted here that Assam is also the home of Tai or Thai speaking people which is spoken in Karbi Anglong District.

Arunachal Pradesh

To the north of Assam lies the state of Arunachal Pradesh with hilly terrains all around. Arunachal Pradesh shares an international border with Bhutan, China, and Burma. It is the home of various groups and subgroups who speak different Tibeto-Burman and Thai-Chinese languages. Some of the major languages of Arunachal Pradesh are: Adi, Adi Gallong/Gallong, Monpa, Wancho, Tangsa, Mishmi, Miri/ Mishing, Nocte, Tagin, Apatani, Idu-Mishmi, Khamti, Singpho, Deori, Tutsa, Ruga, Tase, Nisi, Sherdukpen, and some lesser known languages such as Puroik also known as Sulung.

Meghalaya

Khasi in Meghalaya along with Jaintia, War and Lyngngam together constitute the only Austro-Asiatic language that links up the Mon-Khmer languages of the Southeast Asia with the Munda languages of central India. Garo which belongs to Bodo-Garo subgroup of the Tibeto-Burman family is spoken in Garo Hills of Meghalaya. Substantial population of Garo also live both in Assam to the north of the Garo Hills and in the district of Bangladesh, and as far to the south of Tripura. It should be noted here that Garo has a number of dialects known by such names as Achick/Munde, A'we, A'beng Matchi, Dual and others. Apart from Khasi and Garo, there are substantial numbers of Hmar and Bete speakers in small pockets in the Jaintia Hills. The capital city Shillong (also capital of undivided Assam) houses almost all the languages of the North-East India as well as other Indo-Aryan and Dravidian languages. Shillong has been a centre of learning and tourism which had attracted people of diverse linguistic groups throughout the country. Thus, it can be termed as the linguistic paradise of North-East India.

Nagaland

To the South-East of Assam and North of Manipur lies the state of Nagaland. It is the home of different Naga tribes who speak different forms of Tibeto-Burman languages which are conceived to be mutually unintelligible. The major languages of Nagaland are Ao, Angami, Rengma, Lotha, Sumi/Sema, Khezha, Sangtam, Chang, Konyak, Phom, Khiamniungan, Chokri, Sangtam, Yimchunger, Zeme, and Liangmai. All these languages are introduced in schools as mother tongue or first language from pre-primary level. Kuki, which is spoken by few number of population is also treated equally with other Naga languages and is taught as first language for Kuki speaking children from pre-primary to class VIII. It is to be noted here that, Nagamese, a pidgin, which is now creolized, is a form of Assamese. It is used as a lingua franca for inter-groups communication throughout the state of Nagaland.

Tripura

Still further to the south lies the state of Tripura. Kokborok (formerly known as Tipra or Tripuri) along with Riang (also called Bru) which is considered to be a dialect of Kokborok constitutes the largest Tibeto-Burman language spoken in the state. Kokborok which belongs to the Bodo-Garo subgroup of the Tibeto-Burman family was once the most dominant language of the state before they were reduced to minority by Bengali speakers. Apart from Kokborok, there are substantial numbers of closely related "Old Kuki" languages, viz., Darlong, Ranglong, Rangkhol, Chorai, Kaipeng, and Sakhachep, etc., spoken by a small number of speakers. Today, they embraced themselves under a common nomenclature "Hallam". It is to be noted here that Koloi, which is a variety of Kokborok embraced themselves under "Hallam" which is not a linguistic grouping but an ethnic grouping for many ethnic groups in Tripura.

Mizoram

Sandwiched between Myanmar in the east and south and Bangladesh in the east with a total of 630 miles, Mizoram is the home of the Kuki-Chin cluster called 'Kukish' proper by Shafer. These include Lushai or Dulian, Hmar, Pawi, Lakher or Mara, and Kuki tribes. Apart from the Kuki-Chin languages, there are sizable population of Riang and Chakma spoken in the state. According to 2001 census of Mizoram state Chakma is spoken by 1,76,458 speakers.

Sikkim

Sikkim is the landlocked state located in the Himalayas. It is the least populous state in India and second smallest in area after Goa. Sikkim was an independent state ruled by Chogyal monarchy until 1975, when a referendum to make it India's twenty second state succeeded. Sikkim shares an international border with Nepal in the west, the Peoples Republic of China to the north and east, Bhutan in the south-east and West Bengal to its south from the Indian side. The official language of the state is Nepali. Other major languages include Bhutia,

Lepcha, Limboo, Gurung, Sherpa, Tamang, Newari, Hindi and English. The predominant religions are Hinduism and Vajrayana Buddhism. Gangtok is the capital and largest town.

Manipur

To the south of Nagaland lies the state of Manipur which shares an international border with Myanmar. The Meiteis/Manipuris, Kukis and Nagas together constitute the Tibeto-Burman group in the state. Apart from these three Tibeto-Burman subgroups, there are substantial numbers of Indo-Aryan and Dravidian speakers in different parts of the state. (See for detailed discussion on the languages of Manipur in the Chapter 4).

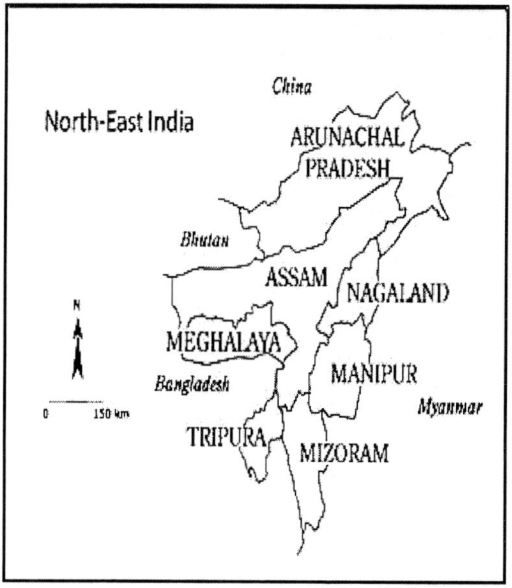

Fig. 1: Map of North-East India

1.1. PROBLEMS OF LISTING THE LANGUAGES OF THE NORTH-EAST INDIA

In addition to the major linguistic groups in the North-East India, viz., Tibeto-Burman, Indo-Aryan and Austro-Asiatic, there are some languages and lingua francas used in inter-lingual contact situations which are not even documented. The languages of the North-East cannot be counted primarily because the region is linguistically unexplored and the knowledge about them is too scanty. The estimated number of languages spoken in North-Eastern India runs as high as two hundred (Downs, 1994), but others suspect that this figure might have been reached by including many mutually intelligible dialects as separate languages. Some of the problems of listing the languages of the North-Eastern India are discussed as follows:

Firstly, many North-Easterners do not differentiate between language and tribe. To them, each tribe is presumed to have its own language, and each language is presumed to be spoken by just one tribe. This presumption comes about because of the fact that by tradition tribes and languages are called by the same names. For example, Angami is spoken by Angami tribe, Garo is spoken by Garo tribe, Khasi is spoken by Khasi tribe, Mizo is spoken by Mizo tribe and so on throughout all the hundred or so languages that are spoken in the North-East. The tradition of naming a language according to each tribe is not true all the times. In North-East India, many people speak language(s) to which they may or may not have tribal membership. Burling (2007) explained how the Rabha living in the low country just north of the Garo Hills, between the hills and the Brahmaputra river are comfortably bilingual and are able to use both the Indic languages of the Assamese and their own Tibeto-Burman Rabha. "Other Rabhas, however, speak only Assamese. Perhaps their grandparents or great-grandparents once spoke Rabha, but the grandchildren do not. They regard themselves as Rabhas and are so regarded by their neighbours, but they violate the expectation that language and tribal membership will always correspond."

Secondly, the difficulty in listing the languages of North-East comes from the fact that, many mutually intelligible dialects are classified as separate languages on the one hand and different speech forms which are conceived to be mutually unintelligible under a single language on the other. This is on account of the fact that the North-Easterners usually give different meaning for what linguists would called 'dialects' (forms of speech that are mutually intelligible) and 'languages' (forms of speech having autonomous system). For them, whatever is spoken by a 'tribe' is likely to be called a 'language', and whatever is spoken by a 'sub-tribe' is a 'dialect'. But this is not true all the time. Sometimes, understandability does not correspond to recognized tribal boundaries. (See section 4.3.2. of chapter 4 for further discussion)

Not only listing the languages of the North-East is also complicated, but the groups and subgroups by which they are called are often confusing because of the changing nomenclatures. Many of the tribal names given by the British have been changed after the independence. Thus, the people formerly known as Lushai came to be known as Mizo, the Mikir came to be known as Karbi, and the Miri became to be known as Mising. Other groups such as Rabhas and Koch, formerly regarded as separate tribes realigned themselves under the slogan 'Rabha are Koch, Koch are Rabha' (Burling, 2003). For long time, most of the indigenous people of Nagaland, together with some ethnic groups in the neighbouring areas of Manipur, Assam, Arunachal Pradesh, and Myanmar have been taken for granted as a linguistic subgroup until recently when Burling (2003) suggested that "The languages spoken by 'Nagas' fall into at least two, and more possibly several, completely distinct branches of Tibeto-Burman." Burling opines that the recognition of 'Naga' ethnicity may have come after the British gave the name 'Naga'. But this term should not befool us in believing that they must have same linguistic family group.

1.2. PROFILE OF THE MAJOR LANGUAGES OF THE NORTH-EAST INDIA

This section deals with the profile of some major languages of North-East India pertaining to their geographical location, population, domain of language used and some scholarly works. For those languages whose figures are not available from Census of India, they are taken from Ethnologue. (See chapter 4 for the language profile of Manipur).

Assamese

Assamese is the official state language of Assam. It is a link language for various linguistic groups across the state. The language is also spoken in the neighbouring states of West Bengal, Meghalaya, Arunachal Pradesh, Nagaland and in the neighbouring countries of Bangladesh and Bhutan. The total population of Assamese speakers is 1,31,68,484 (Census of India 2001). The alternate names are

Asambe, Asami, Asamiya, Jharwa (Pidgin), Mayang, Standard Assamese, Western Assamese. Assamese belongs to Indo-Aryan family of the Indo-European. Assamese script is used as their writing system.

Nagamese

Nagamese a pidgin form of Assamese is widely used in inter-groups communication in the state of Nagaland. A variety farthest from Assamese is spoken by the Yimchenger Naga, and varieties closest to Assamese by the Angami Naga, and around Dimapur and Kohima. The total number of people who speak Nagamese is 30,000 (Ethnologue, 2005). It is used by most of the 5,00,000 speakers of 29 Naga languages as second language. Though Nagamese is not used as a subject of instruction, it is used as teaching medium, i.e. teaching language in schools of Nagaland.

Bishnupriya

Bishnupriya is an Indo-Aryan language mainly spoken in the Assam districts of Cachar, Hailakandi and Karimganj. The speakers are also found to live in North Tripura district and in Bangladesh. For a long time, Bishnupriya had been regarded to be a Bengali-Meitei Creole. But recent studies reveal that it retains pre-Bengali features (Masica, 1991) and is closer to both Bengali and Assamese. The total population of Bishnupriya is 77,545 (Census of India, 2001). It is also known by various names such as Bisna Puriya, Bishnupria Manipuri. The speakers use Assamese and Bengali scripts. The most notable academic work in the language is that of Kim, Amy and Seung Kim. 2008. *"Bishnupriya (Manipuri) speakers in Bangladesh : a sociolinguistic survey."*

Khasi

Khasi is spoken mainly in the state of Meghalaya. The speakers are also found in the district of Cachar, Nowgong, Lakhimpur, and Kamrup District in Assam. Khasi is also spoken in parts of Manipur; West Bengal; Tripura and also in Bangladesh. The total population of Khasi is 11,28,575 (Census of India, 2001). The alternate names are Khaasi, Khasiyas, Khuchia, Kassi, Khasa, and Khashi. The different dialects of Khasi are Bhoi-Khasi, Lyngngam (Megam), War, Cherrapunji (Sohra), Khynrium. Bhoi is spoken in Nongpoh block and Nonglung in East Khasi Hills. Lyngngam dialect in Mawshynrut block in West Khasi Hills is divergent and may not be a dialect (Abbi : 1997). War (Amwi) is a separate language (B. Comrie, 1989). Khasi is the official regional language of Meghalaya and used in administration, mass media, newspapers, radio programmes and in television. The language is taught in primary schools in Roman script. Some of grammatical works include:

1. K.S. Nagaraja, Poona, 1978. "*Descriptive Analysis of Khasi*".
2. K.S. Nagaraja, CIIL, 1990. "*Khasi Phonetic Reader*".
3. K.S. Nagaraja, CIIL, 1994. "*Khasi dialects : a typological consideration*".
4. K.S. Nagaraja, CIIL, 1996. "*The Status of Lyngngam*".
5. I.M. Simon, 1997. "On first looking into Paul K. Benedict's Sino-Tibetan".
6. Alves, J. Mark, 2001. "*Distributional properties of causative verbs in some Mon-Khmer languages*". Khasi Bible "Ka Testamen Barim Bad Ba Thymmai" was translated around 1891.

Garo

Garo along with a number of dialects such as A'we, A'beng, Matchi, Dual etc. is spoken in western half Meghalaya also known as of Garo Hills. The speakers of Garo also live in Assam districts of Goalpara, Kamrup and Karbi-Anglong and Mymensing district of Bangladesh, which all skirt the Garo Hills. Van Driem (2007) located the Garo speakers even further to the south of Bangladesh hinterland about 15,000 in Modhupur. Garo speakers also live in Nagaland, south Tripura district, Jalpaiguri and Cooch Behar districts in West Bengal. The total population of Garo is 8,89,479 (Census of India 2001). General level of education is low compared to Khasi. They use Roman script as their writing system. The language is taught in primary schools.

The most notable grammatical works in the language include:

(1) Mason, C. Marcas, *et al.*, Shilong, 1905. "*English-Garo-Dictionary*".

(2) D.S. Nengminza, Tura, 1946. "*The School Dictionary* (*Garo into English*)".
(3) Burling Robins, Deccan College, Pune, 1961. "*A Garo Grammar*".
(4) R.G. Momin, Tura, 1968. "*English-Garo-Dictionary*".
(5) Marak, W. Harendra, Guahati, 1975. "*Ku'bidik:*"
(6) Marak, W. Harendra, Guahati, 1975. "*Ku'bidik : A Garo-English-Assamese Dictionary*".

Bodo

Bodo is the only Tibeto-Burman language to be included under the Eighth Schedule after Manipuri. It is also the official language of the recently created Bodoland Territorial Council. Bodo is primarily spoken in the entire lower Assam stretching up to Jalpaiguri and Cooch-Behar districts of north Bengal and in the upper districts of Dhimaji, Lakhimpur, Nagaon, Sonitpur, Karbi-Anglong. The Bodo also live in Tikrikilla block of west Garo Hills in Meghalaya and in Jhapa district in Nepal. The language is spoken by 13,50,478 people (Census of India 2001). Bodo has adopted Devanagari script as their writing system.

Some of the grammatical works in the language include:

(1) D.N.S. Bhat, Deccan College, Pune, 1968 "*Bodo Vocabulary (with a grammatical sketch*)".
(2) P.C. Bhattarcharya, Guwahati, 1977, "*A Descriptive Analysis of Bodo Language*".
(3) Mochari, Moniram. Bengtol (Assam), 1985. "*Bodo-English Dictionary*".

Koch

Koch which includes Rabha, and other small Koch languages such as Pani Koch, Wa'nang, Tintikia and Mandai is considered to be dying out. A'tong and Moribund Ruga also belong to the Koch sub-group. It is spoken in west Garo Hills district of Meghalaya, Assam, Tripura, West Bengal, Bihar and in Bangladesh. The population of Koch is 31,119 (Census of India, 2001). Koch of Meghalaya can speak Bengali, Assamese. Educated youths can speak English and Hindi. The speakers use Assamese script.

Rabha

Rabha is spoken in Darrang, Goalpara and Kamrup districts of Assam. The language is also spoken in Nagaland; East Garo Hills district of Meghalaya; and in Jalpaiguri and Cooch Behar districts in West Bengal. The total population of Rabhas according to Census of India 2001 is 1,64,770. The different dialects of Rabhas are Maitaria (Maituri, Maitoria), Rangdania (Rongdani). Maituri and Rongdania have inherent intelligibility to each other's speakers. There is a third dialect called Koch Rabha, spoken in Assam close to West Bengal border. It is not intelligible with Rongdania (Fr. Jose, 2002). The majority of the ethnic groups speak Assamese as their first language and the rest speak Rabha as their first language. Rongdani is the standard dialect but is almost dying out. Most Rabha are bilingual in Assamese and they use Assamese script. The language is also used in radio programmes and in television. The major works is that of U.V. Joseph, Guwahati, 2002. "*Rabha-English Dictionary: Khúrangnala*".

Dimasa

Dimasa is another major language of Bodo-Garo subgroup of the Tibeto-Burman family spoken in the state of Assam. In Assam, Dimasa is mainly spoken in the districts of Cachar, Karbi Anglong, Nowgong and N.C. Hills of Assam. It is also spoken in Nagaland. It should be noted here that the term Hill Kachari was employed in the past literatures to refer to those Dimasas living in N.C. Hills and in and around Nagaland. And those Dimasas living in parts of Nagaon in regions like Longkah, Hojai, Khampur, etc. are known as plain Kacharis or simple Hojai Kacharis. Another name for the Dimasas living in and around Cachar district such as, Silchar and Hailakandi is Rohini Kachari. The total population of Dimasa speakers according to Census of India, 2001 is 1,11,961. Recently, Dimasa was introduced up to class 2 in the primary schools of Assam. The Dimasa have been writing in Assamese, Benglai and Devanagari scripts. Now, under the pressure from the Dimasa literary society and the demand of the younger generation, use of Roman script is increasing day-by-day. Some of the existing literatures include: Thaosen, Sonoram, Haflong, 1994. "*Dimasa Bhasha Bijnan Parichay* (*in Bengali*)".

Rajbanshi

Rajbangshi is spoken in the western part of Assam and in the entire North Bengal. It is an Indo-Aryan language with a higher influence of Bodo group of the Tibeto-Burman family. The total population of Rajbongshi is 82,570 (Census of India 2001). Rajbongshi is also known by various names such as Kamtapuri, Rajbangsi, Rajbansi, Rajbongshi, Tajpuri. The first treatment of Rajbangshi language was by Grierson in his LSI, where he named it the "Rajbangshi dialect of Bengali". Assamese is spoken by the Rajbanshi in Assam. The language is used in poetry, magazines, and videos. Some literatures available in the language include dictionary and "*A Sketch of the Phonology and Grammar of Rajbanshi*" by Wilde, Christopher P. 2008.

Tiwa

Tiwa or Lalung as it is known is spoken in Kamrup, and Morigaon Sibsagar and Lakhimpur districts of Assam. The language is also spoken in Karbi-Anglong district formerly known as 'Mikir Hills'. Tiwa is also spoken in Khasi Hills district of Meghalaya. The total population of Tiwas is 27,960 (Census of India, 2001). The Tiwas are currently using Assamese script. Some of the literatures in the language include dictionary and grammar. The New Testament is also translated into the language.

Deuri

Deuri is spoken in Lakhimpur, Dhemaji, Tinsukia, and Jorhat districts of Assam. The population of Deuri is 27,960 (Census of India, 2001). Most Deuri are bilingual in Assamese but women, older and uneducated people are observed to have less proficiency in Assamese. The speakers are currently using Roman script as their writing system.

Miri/Mishing

It is spoken in North Lakhimpur, Sonitpur, Dhemaji, Dibrugarh, Sibsagar, Jorhat, Golaghat and Tinsukia districts of Assam. In Arunachal Pradesh, it is spoken in Lower and Upper Subansiri district, Ziro subdivision and a few villages near Pasighat, on both sides of the Kamla River and Daporizo subdivision. The Hill Miri in Arunachal Pradesh and the Plain Miri are in Assam. The total population is 4,00,000 (Ethnologue: 2005). The alternate names of the language are Mishing, Mising, Takam. Idu may be its dialect. Grierson classify the language as North Assam group of the Tibeto-Burman family. But, G.D.P. Sastry (1991) prefer to call it as Tani group simply because the speakers prefer to call themselves as "Ami' or "Tani". Speakers use Hindi and Assamese.

Karbi/Mikir

It is spoken in the Karbi-Anglong district of Assam or 'Mikir Hills' as well as in the neighbouring districts of Kamrup, Nowgong and Sibsagar. The total population of Karbi is 4,19,534 (Census of India, 2001). Majority of its speakers are bilingual in Assamese, and amongst the younger generation the ancestral language is being abandoned at an alarming rate in favour of Assamese. Karbi is a Tibeto-Burman language, but its exact place within the group is not yet ascertained.

Kokborok

Kokborok formerly known as 'Hill Tippera' is spoken in the low rolling hills of Tripura. It was once the most dominant language and constitutes at least 70 per cent in the state at the time of India's independence in 1947 from Great Britain and merely 30 per cent were Bengali speakers. Today, the Kokborok constitute just a 30 per cent minority in their own homeland, having been swamped by large scale Bengali immigrants from Bangladesh. Today, the Bengali speakers make up over 85 per cent of the total population of Tripura. The language is also spoken in Assam and in Chittagong Hill tracks of Bangladesh. The various names of Kokborok are Tripuri, Tipura, Usipi Mrung, Tripura, Kakbarak, and Kokbarak. The language is spoken by 8,54,023 (Census of India, 2001). The various dialects of Kokborok are Jamaitia, Koloi, Rupini, Tripura, Noatia, Murasing, Laitong, Uchoi, Riang, Puram, Debbarma. Debbarma is spoken by the royal family and is the medium of communication with the other dialects. It is understood by all, but not *vice versa*. In Tripura, the policy of the state government is to use the Bengali script for all the languages. But the speakers of Kokborok, Chakma and Hallam Kuki also use the Roman script (with some modifications) on informal occasions/in non-official publications.

The most notable works on Kokborok language are:

(1) Pushpa Painee Karapurkar, CIIL, 1976. "*Kokborok Grammar*".
(2) K.S. Francis, Guwahati, 1992. "*English-Kokborok Dictionary*". Bible was translated in 1998.

Riang

Riang or Kau Bru as it is known is spoken in the state of Tripura; Karimganj district in Assam; Aizawl, Lunglei and Chhimtuipui disıricts in Mizoram, mostly along the bank of Karnafuli River. The language is also spoken in Bangladesh. Riang is considered to be a dialect of Kokborok but the Riangs themselves spurn to be identified as Kokborok. It is spoken by 76,450 speakers (Census of India, 2001). Literacy rate is very low. The speakers use Roman and Bengali script. It is said that the Riang of Tripura are different from Riang of Myanmar, a Mon-Khmer language though Muanthanga says they speak a dialect of Kokborok called "Polong-O".

Darlong

Darlong is spoken in Kailashahar and Kamalpur subdivisions of Tripura. The speakers are also found in Bangladesh. The total population of Darlong is 6,000 (Ethnologue, 2005). It is also known by the alternate name Dalong. Darlong belongs to the Central Kuki-Chin subgroup of the Tibeto-Burman family. The speakers use Roman script. The New Testament was translated into Darlong in 1995.

Adi

Adi is spoken in East, West, and Upper Siang districts and in Upper Subansiri and Dibang Valley Districts of Arunachal Pradesh. It is also spoken in Assam. The total population of Adi is 1,98,462 (Census of India, 2001). The alternate names are: Abhor, Abor, Boga'er Luoba, Lhoba, and Luoba. The language may be classified under the Tani group of the Tibeto-Burman family. The speakers also use Assamese,

Hindi, or Nepali. They use Roman script as their writing system. New Testament was translated in 1988.

Adi/Galo

It is spoken in West Siang, East Siang, Dibang Valley (South), Lohit (East), Changlang (North-East), and some in Upper Subansiri (West) Districts of Arunachal Pradesh. The total population of Adi/Galo is 61,887 (Census of India, 2001). It is known by various names such as Adi, Adi-Gallong, Adi-Galo, Gallong, Galong. The language is reportedly intelligible with other Adi dialects but they are socio-linguistically distinct. The language may be classified under the Tani group of the Tibeto-Burman family. The language is used in homes and villages. Most of the speakers use Hindi and Assamese. English is spoken by the educated and by the younger folk. A few older adults are monolinguals. The speakers use Roman script and the language is also used in Radio programmes.

Apatani

It is spoken in Assam, Nagaland and around seven villages in and around Hapoli and Zirol in Subansiri district of Arunachal Pradesh. The total population of Apatani is 28,422 (Census of India, 2001). The language is also known as Apa. Apatani belongs to Tani group of the Tibeto-Burman family. Speakers use Assamese, Hindi, and Nepali. Literacy rate is very low. The most notable work on the language is that of P.T. Abraham, CIIL, 1985. "*Apatani Grammar*".

Idu-Mishmi

It is spoken in Dibang Valley district of Arunachal Pradesh, Assam and West Bengal. The total population of Idu-Mishmi is 33,955 (Census of India, 2001). The language is known by alternate names such as Chulikata, Chulikotta, Ida, Idu, Midhi, Midu, Yidu Luoba. The language is closest to Digaro-Mishmi. Different from Boga'er Lhoba. The language may be classified under the Tani group of the Tibeto-Burman family. The speakers use Assamese and Hindi. Only the educated speak English. Literacy rate is very low. Two most notable works on the languages are: (1) G.D.P. Sastry, CIIL, 1984. "*Mishmi Phonetic Reader*" and (2) G.D.P. Sastry, CIIL, 1984. "*Mishmi Grammar*".

Nisi

It is spoken in Assam, Darrang district, Lower Subansiri and East Kameng districts of Arunachal Pradesh. The total population of Nisi is 1,18,111 (Census of India, 2001). The alternate names are "Dafla", "Daphla", Nissi, Nishi, Nyising, Nyishi, Bangni, Lel. The different dialects are Aka Lel, Bangni, Tagin, Nishang. Nisi is related to Apatani, Adi and Yano. Tagin may be a separate language. The language may be classified under Tani group of the Tibeto-Burman family. Nisi has been used as a cover term for the western Tani languages. The name "Dafla" means 'wild man' and is considered derogatory. The speakers use Assamese script.

Nocte

Nocte is spoken in Khonsa, Namsang and Laju circles in Tirap district and in Changlang District of Arunachal Pradesh. The speakers are also found to live in Lakhimpur district of Assam and in Mon district of Nagaland. The total population of Nocte is 32,957 (Census of India, 2001). The alternate names of Nocte are Borduria, Jaipuria, Mohongia, Namsangia, Nocte, and Paniduria. The language may be classified as Bodo-Konyak sub-group of the Tibeto-Burman family. Assamese or Hindi is used mostly by young and educated people. Others speak Assamese only for trade. English is used by educated office workers. The language is used in Radio programmes too.

Wancho

Wancho is spoken in south-eastern Tirap district of Arunachal Pradesh. It is also spoken in Assam and Nagaland. The language may be classified as Bodo-Konyak sub-group of the Tibeto-Burman family. The total population is 49,072 (Census of India, 2001). The alternate names are Wancho, Banpara Naga, and Joboka. The major dialects are Changnoi, Bor Muthun (Bor Mutonia), Horu Muthun and Kulung Muthun (Mithan). There is a significant variation between the language spoken in the upper regions and the lower ones. Wancho is close to Chang Naga and Konyak Naga. The younger generation speaks Hindi or Assamese as second language. The speaker use both Roman and Devanagari scripts. New Testament was translated in 2002.

Tutsa

Tutsa is spoken in South Changlang and East Tirap districts of Arunachal Pradesh. Their total population is 25,000 (Ethnologue, 2005). It is also known by the alternate names Totcha or Tutsa. The language may be classified under Bodo-Konyak sub-group of the Tibeto-Burman family. The language is used mainly in homes and in villages. The speakers of the language consider themselves separate from Nocte and Tase. Assamese is spoken by young people; Hindi by young and slightly educated people and English by educated young people. Literacy rate in second language is very low.

Monpa

It is spoken in Tawang and West Kameng districts of Arunachal Pradesh. In China the speakers of the language are found to the east of Bhutan, partly in south-eastern Tibet, mainly on the Yarlung-Zanbo River, Medog, Nyinchi, Cuona counties. The total population of Monpa is 55,876 (Census of India, 2001). The alternate names of the language are: Monba, Mompa, Monpa, Momba, Menba, Men-Pa. The various dialects are Matchopa Nagnoo (But), Chug, Sangla (Dirang), Kalaktang (Southern Monpa), Kishpignag (Lish), Monkit (Northern Monpa, Tawang). The Lish, But, and Chug dialects differ from the others, resembling Aka, Miji, and Sherdukpen languages (Singh). Monpa is identical or closely related to Cuona Monpa in Tibet and Brokpa and Brami of Bhutan (Andvik, 2002). The language may be classified under the Kiranti group of Tibeto-Burman family. The speakers use Devanagari script. The language is used in Radio programmes.

Sherdukpen

Sherdukpen or Ngnok as it is known is Tibeto-Burman language spoken mainly in the villages of Rupa, Shergaon, and Jigaon in the south-western corner of Kameng district, but are also settled in area in and around the Tenga valley south of Bomdila. Culturally, the Sherdukpen are distinct from the other Kho-Bwa language communities because they have adopted a Tibetan Mahayana Buddhist *Hoch-kultur* (Van Driem, 2007). The total population is 3,100 (Ethnologue, 2005). The different dialects of Sherdukpen are: Bugun

(Khoa), Lishpa and Butpa might be related, but are little-known languages (Sun Tianshin Jackson, 1993). Speakers also use Hindi or Tshangla.

Puroik

Puroik or Sulung as it is known is spoken by a small hill tribe in the north-eastern hills of East Kameng, Papum Pare and north-western hills of Lower Subansiri districts, along the Par River of Arunachal Pradesh. They are scattered over the nine administrative circles of East Kameng district, viz., Chayangtajo, Pipu, Pakke Kessang, Lada, Bameng, Seijosa, Seppa, Sawa, Khenewa and Pipu-Dipu circles. The language does not seem to share affinity with the neighbouring tribes like, Aka, Nyishi and Maji except for the shared vocabulary and areal features. However, they are said to share a mutually intelligible language with the Khowas (Bunguns) of the West Kameng district (Remsangpuia, 2008). The total population of Puroik is 5,443 (Census of India, 1991). The position of Puroik within the Tibeto-Burman sub-group of family is not yet known for the very reason that no Tibeto-Burmanist has ever attempted to classify the language within any sub-group.

Khamti

Khamti is spoken in Lakimpur district of Assam; Siang and Lohit districts of Arunachal Pradesh and in North-western Myanmar. The population of Khamti according to Census of India, 1991 is 8,462. The alternate names are: Kham-Tai, Hkamti, Khampti, Khamti Shan, Khantis, Tai Kham Ti. Khamti is said to have a number of dialects as Assam Khamti, North Burma Khamti, Sinkaling Hkamti. In India Khamti is related to Phakaes, Aiton, Khamjang, and Turung. The language may be classified as Tai-Kadai, Kam-Tai, Be-Tai, Tai-Sek, Tai. In Myanmar speakers also use Burmese or Jingpho. Academic publications include: Robinson, Edward Raymond. 1994. *Further Classification of Southwestern Tai "P" Group Languages.*

Ao

Ao is one of the largest Tibeto-Burman languages spoken in the state of Nagaland. It is mainly spoken in the central Mokokchung district and parts of Assam. The language belongs to Kuki-Chin-Naga sub-group of the Tibeto-Burman family. The major dialects of Ao are Mongsen, Changki, and Chungli which are said to be mutually unintelligible. The language is spoken by 2,61,387 speakers (Census of India, 2001). The speakers also use Assamese, English, Naga Pidgin or Hindi. They use Roman script as their writing system. Some of the notable grammatical works in the language are:

(1) K.S. Gurubasave Gowda, CIIL, 1975. "*Ao-Grammar*".
(2) K.S. Gurubasave Gowda, CIIL, 1985. "*Ao-English-Hindi Dictionary*".
(3) K.S. Gurubasave Gowda, CIIL, 1992. "*Ao-Naga Phonetic Reader*".
(4) E.W. Clark, Gian Publication, Delhi, 1981e. "*The Ao-Naga Grammar with Illustrations, Phrases and Vocabulary*".
(5) A.R. Coupe, Pacific Linguistics (No. 543), Canberra:2003, "*A Phonetic and Phonological Description of Ao*". Bible was translated in 1964.

Angami

Angami is spoken in western Nagaland and in Kohima district. But in recent times, the language became to be known as Tenyidie. Angami belongs to Kuki-Chin-Naga sub-group of the Tibeto-Burman family. Other alternate names include Gnamei, Ngami, Angamis, Tsoghami, Tsugumi, Monr, and Tsanglo. Naga Chokri and Naga Kezhama are eastern Angami groups with their own dialects. Tenyidie is the standard dialect and is understood by all. There are 2 southern varieties, viz., Viswemal and Jakhama that are not intelligible. The total population of Angami speakers is 1,32,225 (Census of India, 2001). Speakers also use English, Naga Pidgin, or Hindi. Most young people read Angami. Literacy among older people is lower. The speakers use Roman script. Magazines, Dictionary and grammar books are also available in the language.

Some notable works in the language include:

(1) N. Ravindran, CIIL, 1974. "*Angami Phonetic Reader*".
(2) P.P. Giridhar, CIIL, 1980. "*Angami Grammar*".
(3) P.P. Giridhar, CIIL, 1987. "*Angami-English-Hindi Dictionary*". Bible was translated in 1970.

Chang

Chang belongs to Bodo-Konyak sub-group of the Tibeto-Burman family of languages. It is spoken in thirty-six villages in Tuensang District in East Central Nagaland. The population of Chang is 62,408 (Census of India, 2001). The language is close to Wancho. Dialect of Tuensang village is most intelligible to all. The various names of Chang are Mojung, Machongrr, Mochumi, Mochungrr, and Changyanguh. Speakers also use Naga Pidgin, Ao, Assamese, English, or Hindi. The speakers use Roman script as their writing system. New Testament was translated in 1982.

Konyak

Konyak is another language which falls under the Bodo-Konyak sub-group of the Tibeto-Burman family. It is spoken in Sibsagar district of Assam and in Mon and Tuensang Districts in Nagaland. The total population of Konyak is 2,48,109 (Census of India, 2001). The major dialects are Angphang, Hopao, Changnyu, Chen, Chingkao, Chinglang, Choha, Gelekidoria, Jakphang, Kongon, Longching, Longkhai, Longmein, Longwa, Mohung, Tableng, Mon, Mulung, Ngangching, Sang, Shanlang, Shunyuo, Shengha, Sima, Sowa, Shamnyuyanga, Tabu, Tamkhungnyuo, Tang, Tobunyuo, Tolamleinyua, Totok. Tableng is standard dialect spoken in Wanching and Wakching close to Phom Naga. The speakers also use Naga Pidgin, English, or Hindi. Literacy rate in first language: 13 per cent (Singh, 1994). The language is taught in primary schools in Roman script. The major works in the language include:

1. K.S. Nagaraja, CIIL, 1994. "*Konyak-Hindi-English Dictionary*".
2. K.S. Nagaraja, CIIL, 1994. "*Konyak Folklore*".
3. K.S. Nagaraja, CIIL, 1997. "*Kinship terms in Konyak Naga*". Bible was translated in 1992.

Khiamniungan

Khiamniungan is spoken in central part of Tuensang district in Nagaland and north-western Myanmar. The total population is 37,755 (Census of India, 2001). The language is also known as Khiamngan, Khiamniungan, Khienmungan, Khemungan, and Kemmungam. The language is classified under Bodo-Konyak sub-group of the Tibeto-Burman family. In Myanmar the speakers of the language are referred to by the alternate names such as Makware, Nokaw, Para, Ponyo, and Welam. The speakers use Roman script. New Testament was translated in 1981.

Phom

Phom is spoken in 36 villages in Longleng subdivision of Tuensang district in Nagaland. The total population is 1,22,508 (Census of India, 2001). The alternate names are Phom, Phon, Tamlu Naga, Chingmengu, and Tamlu. The language is classified under Bodo-Konyak sub-group of the Tibeto-Burman family. The speakers also use Naga Pidgin. Like most Naga languages the speakers of Phom use Roman script.

The most notable work in the language is that of:

Burling, Robbins and L. Amon Phom, Lingustics of the Tibeto Burman area, 21:43-71, 1999. "*Phom Phonology and Word List*". New Testament was translated in 1978.

Chokri

Chokri is spoken in Phek district of Nagaland, Cheswezumi is the main village. The total population of Chokri is 83,560 (Census of India 2001). Chokri is known by various names such as Eastern Angami, Chakrima Naga, Chakru, Chokri, and Chakhesang. The language may be classified as Angami-Pochuri sub-group of the Tibeto-Burman family. Most Chokris are bilingual in Angami Naga and English. The speakers use Roman script as their writing system.

Sangtam

Sangtham is spoken in Chare Circle and Kiphire subdivision of Tuensang district in Nagaland. The total population of Sangtham is 84,273 (Census of India, 2001). The major dialects of Santham are Kizare, Pirr (Northern Sangtam), Phelongre, Thukumi (Central Sangtam), Photsimi, Purr (Southern Sangtam). Kizare is spoken north of Meluri. It is not known how much it differs from other Sangtam. Santham may be classified as Kuki-Chin-Naga sub-group of the Tibeto-Burman family. The speakers also use Naga Pidgin, Ao, Hindi, or English. Bible was translated in 1995. Chokri, Khezha, and a small section of Sangtam make up the Chakhesang Naga community.

Sumi

Sumi/Sema is spoken in Central and Southern Nagaland. The major settlements of Sumi are in Zunheboto, Kohima, Mokokchung, and Tuensang districts of Nagaland. It is also spoken in seven villages in Tinsukia district of Assam. The total population of Sumi is 1,03,529 (Census of India, 2001). The language is also known as Sema, Simi, and Sumi. The language may be classified as Angami-Pochuri sub-group of the Tibeto-Burman family. The speakers also use Naga Pidgin, Angami, Ao, Lotha, English, or Hindi. The speakers use Roman script as their writing system.

Some of the notable works in the language include:

(1) M.V. Sreedhar, CIIL, 1976. "*Sema Phonetic Reader*".
(2) M.V. Sreedhar, CIIL, 1980. "*Sema Grammar*".
(3) Akilyemiqo, CIIL, 1979. "*Ghenguno Akimi (Tribal Adult Literacy Reader in Sema)*".

Lotha

Lotha is spoken in Workha district in West Central Nagaland. The total population of Lotha is 1,70,001 (Census of India 2001). Lotha is known by various names such as Chizima, Choimi, Hlota, Kyong, Lhota, Miklai, Tsindir, Lutha, Lotha, Tsontsii. The various dialects of Lotha are: Tsontsu, Ndreng, Kyong, Kyo, Kyon, Kyou. The language may be classified as Kuki-Chin-Naga sub-group of the Tibeto-Burman family. The speakers also use Naga Pidgin. The language is taught from primary to class X. The speakers use Roman script as their writing system.

The most notable piece of grammatical work is that of:

K.P. Acharya, CIIL, 1983 "*Lotha Grammar*". Bible was translated between 1967–2000.

Khezha

Khezha live in Phek district in southern Nagaland and in Ukhrul district in North-East Manipur. There are only fourteen Khezha villages which are thickly populated (Kapfo: 2005). Out of the 14 villages, Zhesami in Manipur and Pfüitsero in Nagaland are sub-divisional headquarters. Scholars working on the language in question called Khezha by various names: Grierson (1904) called them Kezhama; Hutton (1921) called them as Kezami or Kezama; Marrison (1967) called them Khezha and Matisoff (1980) explains that the names "Kheja, Kheza and Khezha are co-allograms of the single name referring to a single group. The total population of Khezha is 40,768 (Census of India, 2001). The major dialects include eastern Angami groups with its own language. The language may be classified as Angami-Pochuri sub-group of the Tibeto-Burman. The speakers use Roman script as their writing system.

Some worth mentioning scholarly works in the language are:

(1) Kapfo, CIIL, 2005. "*The Ethnology of the Khezhas and the Khezha Grammar*".
(2) Kapfo, CIIL, 2007. "*Khzhal-Chahale Dikshueri*".

Rengma

Rengma is spoken in Kohima district, and Tseminyu subdivision of Nagaland. The total population of Rengma is 61,345 (Census of India, 2001). The alternate names are Rengma, Rengma Naga, Mozhumi, Moiyui, Mon, Unza, Nzong, Nzonyu, Injang and Southern Rengma. Tseminyu is the main centre for the principal dialect. Southern Rengma and Northern Rengma are reported to be inherently unintelligible to each other. The language may be classified as Angami-Pochuri sub-group of the Tibeto-Burman family. The speakers also use Naga Pidgin or English. The speakers use Roman script as their writing system. Bible was translated in 2000.

Mizo

It is spoken in Mizoram; Assam; Churachandpur district of Manipur; Jampui Hill range, Chittagong Hills Track, Sylhet in Bangladesh and in Western Myanmar. The total population of Mizo is 6,74,756 (Census of India, 2001). The different alternate names are Dulien, Duhlian Twang, Lusai, Lushai, Lusei, Lushei, Lukhai, Lusago, Sailau, Hualngo, Whelngo. Dialects: Fannai, Mizo, Ngente, Tlau, Le. Mizo is related to Hmar, Pankhu, Zahao (Falam Chin), Ralte, Dulien, Le. Mizo belongs to Central Kuki-Chin sub-group of the Tibeto-Burman family. The language is taught till post-graduate. The speakers use Roman script. The language is used in magazines, radio, newspapers, and films. Some of the major works in the language include:

(1) James Herbert, Lorrain. 1940. *Dictionary of the Lushai language*. Calcutta : Royal Asiatic Society of Bengal.
(2) Rochung Buchchwna, Khiangte. 1964. *Lushai grammar*. Aizawl, India: Sinngula.
(3) Remkunga. 1977. *Mizo grammar thar* (New Mizo grammar). Revised. 1984. Aizawl, India: Nazareth Press.
(4) Chhangte, Lalnunthangi (Unpublished M.A Dissertation), University of Texas, Arlington, 1986, "*A Preliminary Grammar of Mizo Language*".
(5) Chhangte, Lalnunthangi, Linguistics of the Tibeto-Burman Area, Vol. 12:1, 1989, "*Complementation in Mizo (Lushai)*". Bible was translated into Mizo between 1959–1995.

Mara/Lakher

It is spoken in around 60 villages in Chhimtuipui district of Mizoram. The language is also spoken in Myanmar. Population of Mara/Lakher is 34,751 (Census of India 2001). The alternate names: Lakher, Zao, Maram, Mira, Mara. The different dialects are Tlongsai (Tlosai-Siaha), Hlawthai. The language is reported to be affiliated with Lai (Haka Chin). Tlosai-Siaha dialect is the lingua franca of all Mara. The language belongs to Kuki-Chin sub-group of Tibeto-Burman. Speakers also use Mizo or English. The speakers use Roman script.

The following tables show the total number of both scheduled and non-scheduled languages spoken in North-Eastern India according to Census of India, 2001.

Table 1: Scheduled Languages of the North-East (Census of India, 2001)

Out of the total 22 scheduled languages, only five languages are spoken in North-East India included under scheduled languages.

Sl. No.	Name	Total number of speakers
1.	Assamese	13,168,484
2.	Bengali	83,369,769
3.	Bodo	12,778,735
4.	Manipuri	1,466,705
5.	Nepali	2,871,749

Table 2: Non-Scheduled Languages of the North-East (Census of India, 2001)

Again, out of 100 non-scheduled languages mentioned in the Census of India, 2001, around 55 languages are spoken in North-East.

Sl. No.	*Name*	*Total number of speakers*
1.	**Adi**	**1,98,462**
	(i) Adi	97,012
	(ii) Adi Gallong/Gallong	61,887
	(iii) Adi Miniyong/Miniyong	17,274
	(iv) Others	22,289
2.	Anal	23,191
3.	Angami	1,32,225
4.	Ao	2,61,387
5.	Gangte	14,500
6.	Garo	8,89,479
7.	Halam	38,275
8.	Hmar	83,404
9.	Kabui	94,758
10.	Kom	14,673
11.	Konyak	2,48,109
12.	Kuki	52,873
13.	Mishmi	33,955
14.	Monpa	55,876
15.	**Nissi/Dafla**	**2,11,485**
	(i) Apatani	28,422
	(ii) Bangni	18,842
	(iii) Nissi	1,18,111
	(iv) Tagin	38,244
	(v) Others	7,866
16.	Nocte	32,957
17.	Paite	64,100
18.	Tangkhul	1,42,035
19.	Tangsa	40,086
20.	Thado	1,90,595
21.	**Tripuri**	**8,54,023**
	(i) Kokbarak	7,61,964
	(ii) Reang	76,450
	(iii) Tripuri	15,002
	(iv) Others	607
22.	Bishnupuriya	77,545
23.	Chakhesang	11,415
24.	Chakru/Chokri	83,560
25.	Chang	62,408
26.	Deori	27,960
27.	Dimasa	1,11,961

(Contd.)

Table 2 *(Contd.)*

Sl.No	*Name*	*Total number of speakers*
28.	English	2,26,449
29.	Karbi/Mikir	4,19,534
30.	**Khasi**	**11,28,575**
	(i) Bhoi Khasi	14,882
	(ii) Khasi	8,28,545
	(iii) Pnar/Synteng	2,43,441
	(iv) War	25,886
	(v) Others	15,821
31.	Khezha	40,768
32.	Khiemnungan	37,755
33.	Lakher	34,751
34.	Liangmei	34,232
35.	Lotha	1,70,001
36.	Lushai/Mizo	6,74,756
37.	Maram	37,340
38.	Maring	22,326
39.	Miri/Mishing	5,51,224
40.	Pawi	24,965
41.	Phom	1,22,508
42.	Pochury	16,744
43.	Rabha	1,64,770
44.	Rai	14,378
45.	Rengma	61,345
46.	Sangtam	84,273
47.	Sema	1,03,529
48.	Sherpa	18,342
49.	Simte	10,225
50.	Vaiphei	39,673
51.	Wancho	49,072
52.	**Yimchungre**	**92,144**
	(i) Tikhi	16,828
	(ii) Yimchungre	72,030
	(iii) Others	3,286
53.	Zeliang	61,547
54.	Zemi	34,110
55.	Zou	20,857

Excludes figures of Paomata, Mao-Maram and Purul sub-divisions of Senapati district of Manipur for 2001 Census.

2

Typological Sketch of Tibeto-Burman Languages of North-East India

2.0. INTRODUCTION

This chapter is an attempt to present a brief typological sketch of the Tibeto-Burman languages of North-East India and should not be in anyway seen as an exhaustive study for typological investigation. Data for the present study is based on the following languages along with author's name and year of publication.

Mising (B.R. Prasad, 1991)
Mishmi (G.D.P. Sastry, 1984)
Angami (P.P. Giridhar, 1980)
Sema (M.V. Sreedhar, 1980)
Lotha (K.P. Acharya, 1983)
Ao (K.S. Gurubasave, 1975)
Khezha (Kedutso Kapfu, 2005)
Phom (R. Burling, LTBA, 1998)
Tangkhul (S. Arokianathan, 1980)
Bodo-Garo (U.V. Joseph and R. Burling, 2006)
Kokborok (P.P. Karapurkar, 1976)
Karbi (V. Y. Jeyapaul, 1987)
Apatani (P.T. Abraham, 1985)
Thadou (M.S. Thirumalai, 1972)
Hmar (P.N. Dutta Baruah, 1996)
Manipuri (C. Yashwanta Singh, 2000)

For the purpose of the present chapter, focus will be made on the vowels and consonants at the phonemic level and exclude all other morphophonemic and syntactic levels for investigation.

2.1. VOWELS

Vowel pattern of the Tibeto-Burman languages of the North-East varies from quite simple five vowel pattern in the case of Garo to ten vowel pattern in the case of Phom. The vowel pattern of the Tibeto-Burman languages of the North-East India is discussed as follows:

Five Vowel Pattern

The basic vowel pattern in Tibeto-Burman languages of the North-East is the five vowel pattern. This vowel pattern is found in Garo and Tiwa as shown below:

i		u
e		o
	a	

U.V. Joseph and Robbins, Burling (2006)

Six Vowel Pattern

A large number of languages have six vowel pattern. This includes Angami, Tangkhul, Apatani, Sema, Ao, Boro and Rabha. Angami, Tangkhul and Manipuri have the same pattern, Apatani and Sema have another pattern, and Ao-Naga, Boro and Rabha have another type of vowel pattern. This may be shown as below:

Angami, Tangkhul and Manipuri

i		u
e	ə	o
	a	

P.P. Giridhar (1980), *S. Arokianathan (1980) and C. Yashwanta Singh* (2000)

Apatani and Sema

i	ɨ	u
e		o
	a	

P.T. Abraham (1985) *and M.V. Sreedhar* (1980)

Ao, Boro and Rabha

i	ɯ	u
e		o
	a	

K.S.G. Gowda (1975), *U.V. Joseph and Robbins Burling* (2006)

Note: The high back unrounded vowel /ɯ/ in Boro is not as high or as back as the corresponding vowel of Rabha. Similarly, the low vowel /a/ in Boro and Rabha may not be as back as the corresponding low vowel in Ao-Naga.

Mising

i	ï	u
	ë	
e	a	ɔ

B.R. Prasad and D.G.P. Sastry (1991).

Lotha

i		u
e		o
	ə	
	a	

K.P. Acharya (1983)

Seven Vowel Pattern

Kokborok

i	ɯ	u
E	ə	ɔ
	a	

Eight Vowel Pattern

Thadou

i		u
e		o
E	ʌ	ɔ
	a	

M.S. Thirumalai (1972)

Nine Vowel Pattern

Nine vowel pattern is found in Mishmi and Khezha.

Mishmi

i	ɨ	u
eê		oõ
	aã	

G.D.P. Sastry (1994)

Khezha

i	I	u
e		o
E	ü[4]/θ	
	a	

Kedutso Kapfu (2005)

Ten Vowel Pattern

	Phom	
i	ɯ	u
e	ʌ	o
E		ɔ
æ	a	

Robbins Burling, LTBA (1998)

2.2. DIPHTHONGS

The Tibeto-Burman languages of North-East India in general have oral diphthongs. The number of diphthongs varies from language to language. Examples from few languages are given below:

Mising has two diphthongs as shown with examples below:
/au/ /mauri/ 'stick used for driving cows', /kauri/ 'shell'
/ɔi/ /jɔitɔ/ 'to put down', /kɔiri/ 'to make rope'

Angami has six diphthongs:
/ei/ /ziesa/ 'sheath', /úphie/ 'lungs'
/əi/ /təirə/ 'rain', /pfenəi/ 'clothing'
/io/ /niô/ 'son', /phihió/ 'to be lame'
/eo/ /deoba/ 'sunday',
/uo/ /úluo/ 'navel', /khruôhì/ 'help'
/ou/ /phikoù/ 'shoe', /toupfə/ 'to carry on back'

Thadou has four diphthongs:
/ai/ /gai/ 'pregnant'
/au/ /hau/ 'yawn'
/ɔu/ /kɔu/ 'ghost/vampire'
/ie/ /nien/ 'dirts'

Khezha has six diphthongs which never occur initially unless uttered in single word as in :

ei/ 'okay' or /ai/ 'it can't be possible'

/ie/	/kenìemí/	'rich people'
/io/	/nìopfo/	'a kind of bamboo basket'
/iu/	/niuj /	'milk'
/ia/	/keniató/	'to fine'
/ei/	/dìe/	'big'
/ai/	/lài/	'an interrogative marker'

Phom has six diphthongs:

/ay/	/phay/	'meat'
/^y/	/l^y/	'come back'
/aɯ/	/haɯ/	'hot/spicy'
/^ɯ/	/c^ɯ/	'fat/grease'
/aw/	/daw/	'grab and pull'
/oy/	/hoy/	'call'

2.3. NASALISED VOWELS

The only Tibeto-Burman language of the North-East which has nasalised vowels under the present study is Mishmi. They are /ẽ/, /õ/ and /ã/.

2.4. CONSONANTS

On the basis of manner of articulation, consonants in Tibeto-Burman languages of North-East India may be divided into stops, nasals, fricatives, affricates, laterals, trill/flaps and semi-vowels. These sounds may differ in their places of articulation. Depending on phonation, these sounds may be further classified into voiced and voiceless sound and according to voice onset time they be classified as aspirated or unaspirated or pre-aspirated.

Stops

At least three stop series consisting of voiceless unaspirated /p, t, k/ voiced unaspirated /b, d, g/ and voiceless aspirated /ph, th, kh/ are the most common pattern found among the stops. The voiceless bilabial stop, voiceless alveolar/dental stop and voiceless velar stop can occur both in the initial and final position. The retroflex sound is generally absent in almost all the languages. The contrast between unaspirated and aspirated voiceless stops is maintained in initial and medial positions. Voicing too is maintained only in initial and medial positions. Most languages allow final but not initial glottal stops. Some of the languages which have at least three series of stops are Angami, Mishmi, Ao-Naga, Boro, Khezha, Lotha, Sema, Tangsa, Tangkhul-Naga, Thadou, Kokborok and Manipuri.

Nasals

Nasal series differ from language to language. The most common among them being the three nasal series /m, n, we ŋ/. This is found in Manipuri, Tangkhul-Naga, Ao-Naga, Thadou and Karbi, Phom, etc. The other three nasal series of the type /m, n, ṅ/ is found in Sema, Apatani and Mishmi. Four nasal series are found of the type /m, n, ñ, ŋ/ is found in Lotha and Mising. The contrast between unaspirated and aspirated nasals is maintained in some Naga languages such as Khezha, Angami and Lotha. Angami distinguishes four unaspirated nasals /m, n, ñ, ŋ/ and three aspirated /mh, nh, ñh/. Lotha distinguishes four unaspirated nasals /m, n, ñ, ŋ/ and four aspirated nasals /mh, nh, ñh, ŋh/. Khezha has three unaspirated nasal /m, n, ŋ/ and two aspirated nasals /mh, nh/.

Fricatives

The number of fricatives varies from one in the case of Mising to nine in the case of Khezha. The only fricative sound in Mising is /z/. Two fricative series are of two subtypes. The first subtype with /f/ and /š/ is found in Mao-Naga and the other subtype having /s/ and /z2 occurs in Ao-Naga. Three fricatives series of the type /s, x, h/ is found in Apatani. Four fricative series of the type /s, z, x, h/ is found in Mishmi and Thadou. Five fricative series are also of two subtypes. The first subtype with /f, s, z, x, h/ is found in Sema while the other subtype with /f, s, z, š, h/ is found in Tangkhul. Seven fricative series of the type /f, v, s, z, š, ž, h/ is found in Lotha and Angami while eight fricative series of the type /f, v, s, z, š, ž, h, ĥ/ is found in Khezha.

Affricate

The affricate series varies in numbers as well in articulation. They are (1) voiceless unaspirated affricates, (2) voiced unaspirated affricates, (3) voiceless aspirated affricates, and (4) voiced aspirated affricates. The following languages, namely Mising, Ao-Naga, Sema and Tangkhul have one affricate each, namely the voiceless alveolar affricate /ts/ in Mising and voiceless palatal affricate /c/ in Ao-Naga, Sema and Tangkhul-Naga. Apatani has two affricates, namely the voiceless palatal affricate /c/ and the voiced counterpart /j/. Karbi has three affricates, namely, the voiceless alveolar affricate /ts/, voiceless aspirated alveolar affricate /tsh/ and voiced alveolar affricate /dz/. Lotha has six affricates which occur in three places of articulation, namely, the labio-dental affricate, alveolar affricate, and palatal affricate. The contrast in aspiration and voicing is shown as below:

/pf/	/ts/	/c/
	/tsh/	/ch/
/pv/		

Angami has nine affricate series at three points of articulation, namely, the labio-dental, alveolar, and palatal. The example below illustrates the contrast in voicing and aspiration in Angami:

/pf/	/ts/	/c/
/pfh/	/tsh/	/ch/
/bv/	/dz/	/j/

Lateral

The lateral series falls broadly into two, unaspirated lateral and aspirated lateral. Languages which have only the unaspirated lateral /l/ are Tangkhul, Karbi, Sema, Apatani, and Mising. Languages which distinguish between unaspirated lateral /l/ and aspirated lateral /lh/ are Ao-Naga, Angami, Lotha and Thadou.

Trill/Flap

Most of the Tibeto-Burman languages of the North-East have trill/ flap sounds /r/. However, languages such as Paite, Thadou and Sema lack either flap or trill sound. The languages which have trill/flap sounds are Karbi, Lotha, Manipuri, Mao-Naga, Mishmi, Mising, Mayon, Tangkhul-Naga, and Kokborok.

Semi-vowel

Semi-vowels /w/ and /y/ are found to occur in number of Tibeto-Burman languages such as Ao-Naga, Mising, Lotha, Mao-Naga, Sema, Tangkhul Naga, Manipuri, and Mishmi. Angami has both unaspirated /w/ and /y/ and aspirated /wh/ and /yh/ semi-vowels, Khezha has two unaspitated semi-vowel /w/ and /y/ and one aspirated semi-vowel /wh/.

2.5. TONE

Most of the Tibeto-Burman languages of the North-East India are tonal except Garo. Languages with three tones are more in number. The languages which have three tones are Ao-Naga, Apatani, Khezha, Karbi, Lotha, Manipuri, Sema, Mising, Tangkhul-Naga, Thadou and Hmar. The three tones are high or rising, mid or level and low or falling.

Languages with two tones belong to the Bodo-Garo languages. According to U.V. Joseph and R. Burling (2006) Tiwa, Boro and Rabha have two tones, namely, high and falling tone. Kokborok which belongs to the same sub-group also has the same tone. Manipuri differs from the Bodo-Garo languages in that it has level and falling tone.

Languages with four tones are Mishmi, Lushai and Mao-Naga. All these languages do not have the same tones. Mishmi has rising, falling, level and rising-falling. Lushai has level, high to low falling, low to high rising and mid to low falling. Mao-Naga has high-level, mid-level, higher-low level and low-level tone.

Angami has five tones, namely, high, mid, mid fall, low fall and low.

2.6. SYLLABLE

The Tibeto-Burman languages of the North-Eastern India are characterized by monosyllabic structure. In most of these languages morpheme boundary corresponds to syllabic boundary. The vowels too are more sonorous than consonants and form peak of the syllable. In a monosyllabic word, with a pattern CVC, the first consonant is called the onset and the second consonant occurring after the vowel is called the coda. Taking a vowel as a peak, the Tibeto-Burman languages of North-East India can have the following syllabic pattern.

Examples of V Syllabic Pattern

Mising	/í/	'blood'
Manipuri	/i/	'blood'
Apatani	/a/	'come'
Thadou	/ú/	'elder brother/sister'
Sema	/ú/	'wear' (cloth)
Karbi	/e/	'yes'

Lotha	/ā/	'my'
Ao	/í/	'wine'
	/ú/	'leave'

Examples of VC Syllabic Pattern

Mising	/ëg/	'yes'
Manipuri	/un/	'skin'
Thadou	/op/	'chest'
Apatani	/iṅ/	'go'
Ao	/ák/	'pig'
Karbi	/an/	'cooked rice, meal'
Sema	/ax/	'gargle' (v)

Examples of CV Syllabic Pattern

Mising	/pë/	'at'
Manipuri	/sa/	'animal'
Thadou	/bù/	'cooked food'
Sema	/ka/	'shoot' (v)
Karbi	/co/	'axe'
Ao	/tí/	'eight'
Apatani	/ma/	'no'

Examples of CVC Syllabic Pattern

Mising	/dëŋ/	'country'
Manipuri	/məŋ/	'dream'
Thadou	/dəŋ/	'palate'
Apatani	/koñ/	'one'
Karbi	/nep/	'catch'
Sema	/hey/	'hammer' (v)
Ao-Naga	/sak/	'open (eyes)'

2.7. CONSONANT CLUSTERS

The consonant clusters of Tibeto-Burman languages of the North-East show two patterns as far as the occurrence of consonant clusters are concerned. The Kuki-Chin languages like Thadou, Paite, Vaiphei, Simte, Gangte, Zou, etc. do not permit clusters word initially and word-finally, rather they permit clusters only in word medial position. Other languages like Karbi, Ao-Naga, Manipuri, Apatani, etc. permit clusters either initially and medially but final clusters are not permitted in almost all the languages of North-East India. In this chapter the discussion of occurrence of consonant clusters will be limited to word initial position only.

Word-initial Consonant Clusters

In initial position consonant cluster up to two consonants are allowed. The second member is always a liquid or semi-vowel and the first member is always a stop or fricative. Given below are the patterns of consonant clusters permitted with the languages and examples from them.

Clusters	Language	Examples
stop+ lateral	Karbi	/plagvuk/ 'a kind of bat', /klem/ 'do'
	Manipuri	/klas/ 'class', /klәp/ 'club'
	Sema	/plakɨthi/ 'coriander seed', /kla/ 'wed'
	Ao-Naga	/plhoŋ/ 'both', /plhaŋpu/ 'gun', /tlhok/ 'six', /tlhonam/ 'scent'
stop+trill	Karbi	/throk/ 'six', /prapjin/ 'fast', 'stout person'
	Manipuri	/tren/ 'train'
	Sema	/krista/ 'christ'
	Mishmi	/prà/ 'virtue'
	Mao	/pràkró/ 'forehead'
	Angami	/prû/ 'jump'
stop+ semi-vowel	Karbi	/gyani/ 'wise person'
	Apatani	/byibu/ 'gun'
	Sema	/kyá/ 'what'
	Khezha	/khwe/ 'wait'
	Manipuri	/kwa/ 'bettal nut', /kyamlәy 'a kind of tree' /khwaŋ/ 'waist'
fricative+semi-vowel	Manipuri	/sway-da/ 'here', /sro-sro/ 'noises'
Nasal+obstruent	Sema	/msa/ 'fear' /mkasɨ/ 'ebony'
Nasal+nasal	Lotha	/nmáthà/ 'to disagree'
Nasal+Lateral	Lotha	/nhrē/ 'crook'

2.8. GENERAL CHARACTERISTICS

The Tibeto-Burman languages of North-East India are rich in suffixes and verbal morphology. Some of the suffixes occur either as a case markers on the nouns or as tense-aspect markers on the verbs. Most of the languages have large numbers of compounds, of which noun compounds are particularly important.

Tibeto-Burman languages are also rich in vocabulary. Slight differences in the varieties of some particular animals are denoted by means of different terms. Many languages of the North-East particularly Mizo, Mishmi, have about twenty different translations of one word 'basket'.

Note: Many Tibeto-Burmanists are of the opinion that the Tibeto-Burman languages have difficulty in forming words for abstract ideas. Thus, Professor Friedrich Mülle of Vienna, in his compendium of Comparative Philology went to the extent of saying that "such languages have no proper comprehension of forms, and are quite unfit for the classification and combination of ideas. The principal reason is that they do not possess particles, i.e. words with a wider meaning, which support the act of thinking like algebraic formulas. When such languages are forced into modern conceptions, as for instance in translating the Bible; they are at once overcome by the substance; they conceive as substance what we conceive as form." (Quoted from LSI, Vol. III, Part III)

3

The Position of Kuki-Chin-Naga within the Tibeto-Burman Family

3.0. INTRODUCTION

Before the British came to India, denominations such as Kuki and Naga were not popularly employed if not unheard of. It appears that the terms Kuki and Naga were coined by British colonial rulers to sooth their colonial motives. Today, our understanding of the two terms suggests that they are of Indo-Aryan origin either Assamese or Bengali with whom they might have come in close contact. Thus, when the British came to India, they borrowed these denominations to differentiate the two groups of people. Later, the two terms were employed in the classification of Tibeto-Burman languages to denote family name(s).

So far as the grouping and sub-grouping of the Kuki-Chin and Naga languages within the Tibeto-Burman family is concerned, there is no one to one agreement among different linguists and the internal relationship between them is still unclear. Different linguists classify the Kuki-Chin and Naga languages differently but no scholar (with all its modifications) is able to come up with a classification which can place all these languages satisfactorily. Most of the classifications we have today are inconsistent and there are various overlappings and contradictions among various linguists in their treatment of the Kuki-Chin and Naga languages.

3.1. CLASSIFICATION OF KUKI-CHIN-NAGA (GRIERSON-KONOW, 1903, 1904)

Grierson and Konow (1904) classified the Kuki-Chin and Naga as separate sub-groups. Grierson-Konow divided the Kuki-Chin languages into four subgroups, viz., Southern-Kuki, Central-Chin, Northern-Chin, and Old-Kuki as shown in Fig. 2 below:

Fig. 2: Classification of Kuki-Chin (Grierson-Konow, 1904)
Kuki-Chin (proper)

- Southern-Kuki
  - Sak
  - Sho
  - Chinbon
  - Chinbok
  - Khami
  - Yindu
  - Pallaing
- Central-Chin
  - Lushei
  - Zahao
  - Tashon
  - Pankhu
  - Haka
  - Banjgi
  - Tlanthang
  - Laker
- Northern-Chin
  - Thado
  - Siyin
  - Paite
  - Ralte
  - Sokte
- Old-Kuki
  - Hmar
  - Chiru
  - Aimol
  - Purum
  - Langrong
  - Chaw
  - Bete

Rangkhol
Hallam
Kolhreng
Kom
Lamgang
Anal
Meithei
Meithei

Grierson-Konow (1903) further divided the Naga languages into five sub-groups: (1) Naga-Kuki sub-group, (2) Naga-Bodo sub-group, (3) Western-Naga sub-group, (4) Central-sub-group, and (5) Eastern-sub-group as shown in Fig 3.

Fig. 3: Classification of Naga (Grierson-Konow, 1903)

Naga-Kuki Sub-group
Maring
Khoibu
Tangkhul
Khangoi
Phadang
Maram
Kwoireng
Liyang
Mao
Sapvoma
Naga-Bodo Sub-group
Kabui
Khoirao
Arung
Empui
Kachcha
Mikir
Western-Naga Sub-group
Rengma
Unza
Mayi
Kezhama

Chakrima
Sema
Simi
Angami
Dzuna
Kehena
Mima
Nali
Tengima

Central-Sub-group

Lotha
Miklai
Yachumi
Yimtsurr
Thukumi
Ao
Chungli
Hatigoria
Mongsen
Tengsa

Eastern-Sub-group

Moshang
Shangge
Monongia
Namsangia
Banpara
Mithan
Tableng
Angwanku
Tamlu
Assiringia
Chingmegnu
Chang
Mojung

Grierson and Konow's classification of Kuki-Chin and Naga languages though extensive in its coverage, has many criss-crossing in their treatment of the Kuki-Chin and Naga languages. Though, Grierson and Konow classification works fairly well for the Kuki-

Chin languages, but when it comes to classifying the Naga languages Grierson and Konow could not ascertain the position of some languages such as Maring, Khoibu, Tangkhul, Kangoi, Phadang, Maram Kwoireng, Liyang, Mao, Sapvoma, Kabui, Khoirao, Arung, Empui, and Kachcha. For example, in the division of the Naga group the term *Naga-Kuki* and *Naga-Bodo* sub-groups are used to club together some of the languages whom Grierson and Konow knew very little about them. Accordingly, they clubbed together Maring, Khoibu, Tangkhul, Kangoi, Phadang, Maram Kwoireng, Liyang, Mao, Sapvoma under the *Naga-Kuki sub-group* and Kabui, Khoirao, Arung, Empui, and Kachcha under the *Naga-Bodo sub-group*. Grierson himself admitted that for the languages of Eastern sub-group, he has been able to do very little beyond collecting previous existing material, much of which was far from accurate. Though, Grierson is of the opinion that, Maring most nearly approaches the languages of the Kuki-Chin group, he still placed it under the Naga group along with Sapvoma or Mao, Maram, Miyangkhang, Kwoireng or Liyang, Luhupa or Luppa, Tangkhul, and Phadang under the sub-group *Naga-Kuki*. The use of the term *Naga-Kuki* and *Naga-Bodo* as constituting a separate sub-group within the super Naga group is misleading and confusing because it is difficult to think of *Naga-Kuki* and *Naga-Bodo* constituting a separate sub-group within the Naga language family.

3.2. CLASSIFICATION OF KUKI-CHIN-NAGA (SHAFER 1955, 1966)

Like Grierson-Konow, Shafer (1955, 1966) also failed to place the Kuki-Chin and Naga languages satisfactorily. But, unlike Grierson and Konow, Shafer elevated Kuki as the super group for all the Kuki-Chin and Naga languages including Meithei and Mikir. Thus, he classified all the Naga languages (except Konyak) under the Kukish section. Shafer elevation of Kukish as the super group to embrace all the Kuki-Chin and Naga languages is equally confusing because the Naga languages are very diverse to form a sub-group within the closely related Kuki-Chin (Kukish) group. Using mostly geographical names he classified these languages into eleven sub-groups, viz., (1) Southern Branch, (2) Central Branch, (3) Northern Branch, (4) Lakher Branch, (5) Old Kuki Branch, (6) Luhupa Branch, (7) Western Branch, (8) Eastern Branch (9) Northern-Naga, (10) Mikir Branch and (11) Meithei Branch as shown in Fig 4.

Fig. 4: Classification of Kuki-Chin-Naga (Shafer 1955, 1966)

- KUKISH
- Southern Branch
  - Sho
  - Sandoway
  - Chinbon
  - Thayetmyo
  - Minbu
  - Chittangong
  - Lamyo
  - Yawdwin
  - Chinbok
  - Khami
  - Khimi
  - Matu
  - Yindu
- Central Branch
  - Lushei Unit
    - Lushei
    - Zahao
    - Pankhu
    - Hmar
  - Haka Unit
    - Haka
    - Shonshe
    - Taungtha
    - Banjogi
  - Kapwi Unit
    - Kapwi
- Northern Branch
  - Thado
  - Siyin
  - Paite
  - Ralte
- Lakher Branch
  - Lakher
  - Sabeu
  - Shandu
  - Zeuhnang

- Old Kuki Branch
  - Central Unit
    - Chiru
    - Aimol
    - Purum
    - Langrong
    - Chaw
  - Western Unit
    - Bete
    - Rangkhol
    - Hallam
    - Southern Luhuppa
  - Lamgang Unit
    - Lamgang
    - Anal
  - Langet
    - Langet
- Luhupa Branch
  - Maring Unit
    - Maring
    - Khoibu
  - Tangkhul Unit
    - Tangkhul
    - Champhung
    - Phadang
    - Ukhrul
  - Kupome Unit
    - Khunggoi
    - Kupome
    - Luhupa
- Western Branch
  - Maram
  - Kwoireng
  - Liyang
  - Kabui
  - Khoirao
  - Arung
  - Empui
- Eastern Branch
  - Rengma Unit

- Rengma
- Anyo
- Nzong
- Nzonyu

Simi (Sema) Unit
- Mao
- Sapvoma
- Kezhama
- Sema
- Dayang
- Simi
- Zuomomi

Angami Unit
- Chakrima
- Angami
- Dzuna
- Kenena
- Mima
- Tengima

Northern Naga

Hlota Unit
- Lotha
- Kyo
- Ndreng

Yatsumi Unit
- Yachumi

Thukumi Unit
- Thukumi

Ao Unit
- Changki
- Chungli
- Khari
- Mongsen
- Tengsa
- Yacham

Mikir Branch
- Mikir

Meilthei Branch
- Meithei

Shafer differs from that of Grierson and Konow in a number of ways: Firstly, Shafer placed some of the languages, viz., Maring, Tangkhul and Kupome under the Lahupa branch. But Grierson and Konow placed them under the sub-group *Naga-Kuki.*

Secondly, Shafer placed, some of the languages, viz., Maram, Kwoireng, Liyang, Kabui, Khoirao, Arung and Empui as separate group under the Western Branch. While Grierson and Konow placed Maram, Kwoireng, and Liyang under the *Naga-Kuki* sub-group and Kabui, Khoirao, Arung and Empui under the *Naga-Bodo* sub-group.

Thirdly, Shafer placed Mao and Sopvoma as part of Simi/Sema unit under the Eastern Branch. But Grierson and Konow placed Mao and Sopvoma under the *Naga-Kuki* sub-group and Simi/Sema under Western-Naga sub-group.

3.3. CLASSIFICATION OF KUKI-CHIN-NAGA (BENEDICT, 1972)

Like Shafer, Benedict (1972) established Kuki (Kukish) as a super group, and placed most of the languages which Shafer calls Lahupa branch under Transition to Naga which includes Tangkhul-Kuki (Maring, Khoibu, Tangkhul), Tangkhul-w Kuki (Poeron), Western Kuki (Mara, Kwoireng, Kabui, Khoirao, Empui). The use of Tangkhul-Kuki, Tangkhul-w Kuki, and Western Kuki are equally confusing if not disturbing. When it comes to the question of classifying the Kuki-Chin and Naga languages, he could not differentiate which of the languages are Kuki types and which are Naga types. Thus, he simply maintained that no sharp linguistic distinction between the Naga and Kuki can be maintained, and hence the two must be placed together under a single rubric (Kuki-Naga). The classification of Kuki-Naga (Kukish) according to Benedict, 1972 is given in Fig. 5.

Fig. 5. Classification of Kuki-Chin-Naga (Benedict, 1972)

KUKISH
- Kuki Proper
  - Southern-Kuki
    - Sho
    - Yawdwin
    - Khami

- Central-Kuki
  - Lushei
  - Haka
  - Lakher
- Northern-Kuki
  - Thado
  - Siyin
- Old-Kuki
  - Aimol
  - Purum
  - Chaw
  - Bete
  - Rangkhol
  - Lamgang
  - Anal
- Transition to Naga
  - Tangkhul-Kuki Type
    - Maring
    - Khoibu
    - Tangkhul
  - Tangkhul-w Kuki
    - Poeron
  - Western-Kuki
    - Mara
    - Kwoireng
    - Kabui
    - Khoirao
    - Empui
- Naga-Proper
  - Southern-Naga
    - Injang
    - Mao
    - Sapvoma
    - Sema
  - Angami
  - Northern-Naga
    - Lotha
    - Ao
- Further from Kuki-Naga

Mikir
    Mikir
Methei
    Meithei

3.4. CLASSIFICATION OF KUKI-CHIN-NAGA (BRADLEY, 1997)

Using Shafer and Benedict's classification as a basis for his classification, Bradley (1997) classified the Kuki-Chin and Naga languages as part of "Kuki-Chin-Naga" group. Although, Bradley (1997) classified Kuki-Chin-Naga languages under the North-eastern India group based on substantial lexical and morphosyntactic similarities, he marks the relationship by dotted line because Shafer classifies it as part of Burmic and Benedict links it to Burmese-Lolo. Despite his detailed picture of the Tibeto-Burman especially at the lower level, Bradley is not able to put the Kuki and Naga languages correctly. For instance, he placed Maring along with the Naga languages and placed it under Southern Naga. The classification of Kuki-Naga according to Bradley (1997) is provided in Fig. 6.

Fig. 6: Classification of Kuki-Chin-Naga (Bradley, 1997)

- Southern Naga
    - Ao
    - Sangtam
    - Yimchungru
    - Nyengi/Meluru
    - Tangkhul
    - Maring
    - Sema
    - Angami
    - Chakhesang
        - Chokri
        - Khezhama
    - Mao
    - Rengma
    - Maram
    - Zeliangrong
        - Mzieme

- Zeme
- Liangmai
- Puiron
- Nruanghmei

Old Kuki
- Meitie
- Rangkhol
- Bete
- Hallam
- Langrong
- Hmar
- Anal
- Kom
- Chawte
- Moyol
- Other Old Kuki

Chin
- Northern
    - Various
- Central
    - Lai (Zo)
    - Mizo
- Southern
    - Asho

Other Chin
- Khami/Khumi
- Mara
- Arleng (Mikir/Karbi)

3.5. CLASSIFICATION OF KUKI-CHIN-NAGA (MATISOFF, 1991, 2001)

Matisoff's (1991, 2001) classification of Tibeto-Burman languages at the lower level has been termed as the most misleading and controversial classification in recent times. Though, Matisoff was himself a contributing editor of Benedict Conspectus (1972), he differs with that of his predecessor (Benedict) in several respects. Matisoff clubbed together all the Kuki-Chin-Naga languages along with Mikir, Meithei and Mru under the same taxonomic order with Bodo-Garo and Abor-Miri-Dafla under the North-east India branch of the super group

Kamarupan. Matisoff's grouping of all the languages of North-eastern India under the term Kamarupan has been criticised by many Tibeto-Burmanists particularly Burling on the ground that it lacked any convincing genetic classification but invited misunderstanding because others, who may have been influenced by the term 'Kamarupan', will presume that the Tibeto-Burman languages of North-eastern India really do form a genetic sub-group. The classification of Sino-Tibetan, (after Matisoff, 1991, 2001) is given in Fig. 7. below:

Fig. 7: Kamarupan

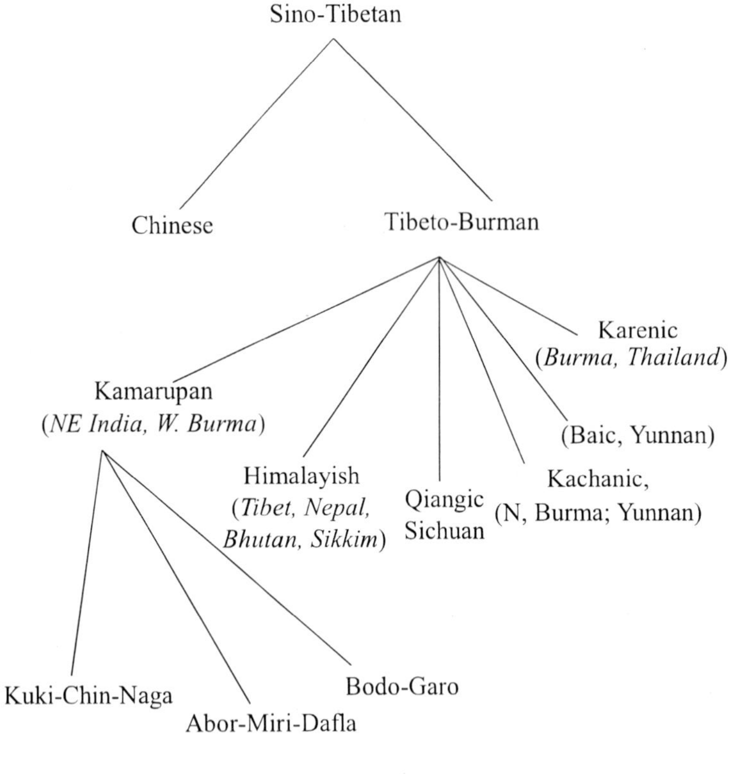

3.6. CLASSIFICATION OF KUKI-CHIN-NAGA (BURLING, 2003)

Burling differs from the earlier classifications in that, instead of using the ethnic names as the name of the language groups or sub-groups, he classifies the languages of North-East India based on geographical location. He is very apprehensive of the use of the term 'Kamarupan' and Baric. Burling is also skeptical of the use of Baric by the International Encyclopedia of Linguistics, a term never before used so widely (DeLancey: 1991). Burling (2003) classified the Tibeto-Burman languages of North-East India into three sub-groups:

1. The Central areas which includes Bodo-Konyak-Jinghpaw.
2. The Northern area which includes: (i) Tshangla-Takpa, (ii) Sherdukpen, Bugun/Khoa, Sulung, Lishpa, (iii) Hrusish, (iv) Tani [Mirish, Misingish, Abor-Miri-Dafla], (v) Idu-Digaru, and (vi) Miju.
3. The Eastern Border areas which includes the Kuki-Chin and the Naga languages: (i) Ao, (ii) Angami-Pochuri, (iii) Zeme, (iv) Thangkhul, (v) Karbi [Mikir], (vi) Meitei, and (vii) Mizo-Kuki-Chin.

Unlike the earlier classifications of Shafer, Benedict, Matisoff etc. Burling (2003) is very apprehensive about the use of the term Naga as forming a genetic sub-group within the Tibeto-Burman language family and avoided the used of the term Kuki-Naga as super-group for all the Kuki, Naga, Mikir and Meithei languages. Instead he calls each group by its prominent language—the Ao group, the Angami-Pochuri group, the Zeme group, Tangkhul group and so on. Burling classification conclusively maintained that Konyak and Chang are affiliated with Bodo-Koch and with Jinghpaw and Mizo-Kuki-Chin form a genetic group.

Burling (2003) classification of the languages of North-eastern India has shed more understandings about the sub-grouping of Kuki-Chin and Naga languages. Firstly, he has rejected the claim that Kuki-Chin and Naga languages along with Meithei and Mikir form a genetic sub-group within the Tibeto-Burman. Secondly, he confidently reaffirms that Kuki-Chin dialects and languages form a branch within Tibeto-Burman. Thirdly, though he is unable to judge how each individual groups relate to each other, he disagrees with most scholars in that the Naga languages fall into at least two, and possibly several completely distinct branches of the Tibeto-Buman. The classification of Eastern Border language by Burling (2000, 2003) is shown in Fig. 8.

Fig. 8: Classification of Eastern Border Languages (Burling 2003)

- Ao Group
  - Yacham-Tengsa
  - Ao-Chungli
  - Ao-Mongsen
  - Sangtham
  - Yimchungru
  - Lotha
- Angami-Pochuri Group
  - Rengma N.
  - Pochuri
  - Rengma
  - Simi
  - Angami
  - Chokri
  - Kheza
  - Mao
- Zeme Group
  - Nruanghmei
  - Puiron
  - Khoirao
  - Zeme
  - Mzieme
  - Liangmai
  - Maram
- Tangkhul Group
  - Tangkhul
  - Maring
- Karbi
- Meithei
- Mizo-Kuki-Chin

In the absence of more reliable classifications, which can place the Kuki-Chin and Naga languages more satisfactorily, we have no option but to rely on them until some more authentic classifications come out. With more and more research studies having made progress in the studies of the Kuki-Chin and Naga languages, it is hopeful that a more reliable classification will be tangible in near future.

4

The Linguistic Situation in Manipur

4.0. INTRODUCTION

Manipur is the home of various Tibeto-Burman languages and dialects. These languages and dialects may be broadly divided into three sub-groups—Meitei/Manipuri, Kuki and Naga. Meitei/Manipuri is by far the largest in terms of its population and size and the only language of the state to be included under the Eighth Schedule of the Constitution of India. Apart from these major linguistic groups, there are substantial numbers of the Indo-Aryan and Dravidian speakers settled in different parts of the state for the purpose of business and trade. The Indo-Aryan and Dravidian speakers are mainly found in Imphal and in the small town of Moreh, an Indo-Burma trade border. Manipur is also the home of *Meitei Pangal* (a name given to Muslim minorities) who are comfortable bilinguals in Manipuri and have been using it as their home language for many decades. The Manipuris and Meitei Pangals are concentrated in and around Imphal Valley, while the Kukis and the Nagas inhibit the hills surrounding the Valley. According to Census of India 2001, there are 29 recognized tribes in Manipur, viz., 1. Aimol, 2. Anal, 3. Angami, 4. Chiru, 5. Chothe, 6. Gangte, 7. Hmar, 8. Kabui, 9. Kacha Naga, 10. Koirao, 11. Koireng, 12. Kom, 13. Lamgang, 14. Mao, 15. Maram, 16. Maring, 17. Any Mizo (Lushai) Tribes, 18. Monsang, 19. Moyon, 20. Paite, 21. Purum, 22. Ralte, 23. Sema, 24. Simte, 25. Suhte, 26. Tangkhul, 27. Thadou, 28. Vaiphei, and 29. Zou. Apart from these recognized languages, there are substantial numbers of Tarao, Kharam and Khezha languages spoken in different parts of the state. Khezha is spoken in Ukhrul district in the north-east Manipur. Kapfo (2005) reports that Zhesami in Manipur and Pfüitsero in Nagaland are the biggest villages of Khezha. On the basis of their relatedness, the languages of Manipur may be divided into two groups—Kuki-Chin group and Naga group. For reason of their similarity, Manipuri, the *lingua francha* of the state has been clubbed under the Kuki-Chin group by Grierson (1930).

4.1. NAGA LANGUAGES

The Naga languages of Manipur like their counterpart Naga languages in Nagaland are quite diversified and are not intelligible to each other. They used Manipuri for inter-language communication both among the Naga tribes as well as with other linguistic groups in the state. Tangkhul is by far the largest and the most described language among the Naga languages in Manipur. David Mortensen (2003) contended that "the Tangkhuls are quite diversified linguistically, and the speech varieties of most Tangkhul villages are not mutually intelligible with those of the neighbouring villages (though the similarities are large enough to facilitate the rapid learning of one another's languages." Brown (1837) also noted that Tangkhul is a group of languages, rather than a single language.

The next important Naga languages of Manipur are—Rongmei, Liangmai and Zeme who are together known as Zeliangrong which is an ethnic nomenclature and not a linguistic grouping. Rongmei or Kabui as it is known is the most dominant language among the Zerianglong cluster. The Liangmai and Zeme are small in size and population. Whatever is known about these languages is that, most Liangmais and Zemeis in Tamenglong district can understand Rongmei but not *vice versa*. It is to be noted here that, Rongmei is mostly spoken in Tamenglong Head Quarters as a result it has become the link language among the Zerianglong cluster. But in other parts of Manipur and elsewhere where they are found to live in isolation, no two speakers of the Zeliangrong can understand each other. The varieties of Rongmei also differ as one goes from North-west to Central parts of Manipur Valley where the speakers are also found to live. But still they are mutually intelligible to one another.

The remaining Naga languages are distributed to the North of the Imphal Valley along the National Highway 39 on the border of Nagaland. These include Mao, Maram and Koiraos (Thangal). Poumai which was considered as part of Mao has been in the lists of tribes to be recognized as separate Scheduled tribe by the government of Manipur.

4.2. KUKI-CHIN LANGUAGES

The Kuki-Chin languages of Manipur may be divided into Old Kuki and Norther Kuki-chin. Grierson classification of Kuki-Chin into Old Kuki and Northern Kuki-chin is adopted here mainly for the convenience of classifying the mutually intelligible languages and dialects from those beyond the range of mutual intelligibility. Accordingly, the Old Kuki groups are: Aimol, Anal, Chiru, Chothe, Koirao, Koireng, Kom, Lamgang, Monsang, Moyon, Purum, Hmar and Tarao. The position of Maring is not well defined. Many Tibeto-Burmanists particularly Grierson is of the opinion that, Maring most nearly approaches the languages of the Kuki-Chin group, but he could not ascertain the position of Maring and simply clubbed it under the same taxonomic order with some languages, viz., Sapvoma or Mao, Maram, Miyangkhang, Kwoireng or Liyang, Luhupa or Luppa, Tangkhul, and Phadang which he classified them under the Kuki-Naga sub-group of Naga languages. Today, the Old Kuki group whose language is a linguist would without hesitation classify then as 'Kuki' have declared themselves to be 'Naga'.

The Northern Kuki-chin languages on the other hand include Gangte, Paite, Simte, Thadou, Vaiphei and Zou. The most dominant among them is Thadou. The name Thadou is a bond of contention for a very long time among the speakers in Manipur. (See section 5.4. of Chapter 5 for detailed discussion).

4.3. PROBLEMS OF IDENTIFYING THE LANGUAGES OF MANIPUR

The problems of identifying the languages of Manipur may be discussed under the following heads:

4.3.1. Shift in Ethnic Loyalty and Political Affiliation

One of the major problems of identifying the languages of Manipur is shift in ethnic or political affiliation from the previous group to the new group. Today, the Old Kuki groups, viz., Anal, Maring, Mayon, Monsang, Lamgang, Chothe, Chiru, Kom, etc. who were once identified as Kuki have now shifted their ethnic loyalty and political affiliation to the new Naga group. But in doing so, they have not shifted their language but have still retained their own languages.

But, when people talked about ethnic affiliation of the group, they talked as if they have shifted their language as well.

4.3.2. Ambiguity in the Distinction of Language and Dialect

Another problem in identifying the languages of Manipur is the ambiguity in the distinction of language and dialect. It is on account of the elusiveness of the distinction between language and dialect that many mutually intelligible dialects of the Kuki-Chin sub-group spoken in the state of Manipur and in the adjoining hills are regarded as separate languages. On the contrary different speech forms of Tangkhul which are conceived to be mutually unintelligible are regarded as belonging to a single language, i.e. Tangkhulon. If, we are to go by pure linguistic criterion, we will give the label *dialects* for the mutually intelligible speech forms of the Kuki-Chin and *separate languages* for the different mutually unintelligible speech forms of Tangkhul. But in many parts of the North East India, the basis for determining whether a particular speech form is a dialect or language depends on tribal membership than linguistic criterion of mutual intelligibility. Thus, so long as people remain under the membership of one tribe they regarded themselves as speaking the language of that tribe. But, the moment they are recognized as separate tribe they will regard themselves to be speaking a separate language.

4.3.3. Profusion and Confusion of Different Names for the Same Languages

The most complicated problem of identifying the languages of Manipur comes from the confusion of different names for the same language. It is on account of such confusion that the speakers of the same language are identified separately as Thadou and Kuki (See Chapter 5 for detailed discussion).

4.4. LINGUISTIC MINORITIES AND ENDANGERED LANGUAGES OF MANIPUR

As Snehamoy Chaklader (1990) has rightly pointed out, that there is no question of linguistic majority or minority at the national level because, if we are to go by the definition of minority as an ethnic community that constitutes less than fifty per cent of the total population of a state, then, India is a land of linguistic minorities. There is not a single linguistic group in India which can claim fifty per cent of the total population of the country. Even Hindi which is recognized as the official language of the Union is not the language of more than one-third of the total population of the country. The question of linguistic minority arises at the state level only. The Supreme Court in 1958 came with a definition when it stated that "minority community means a community which is numerically less than 50 per cent". The Supreme Court further held that when a Bill is passed by the State Legislature which extends to whole of the state, the minority must be determined by reference to the total population of the state. Thus, on the basis of the Supreme Court judgement, we can define linguistic minority as any ethnic group which constitutes less than 50 per cent of the total population of the state and whose mother tongue is different from the language of the majority and the official language of the state. The States reorganization of 1956 with its attempt to reduce the number of linguistic minorities could not do much as in every state there were left a large number of people whose mother tongue is quite different from the language of the majority group.

As it is evident from the Census of Manipur (2001), the percentage of various Scheduled Tribes in Manipur varies from 1.5 in the case of Simte to 24.6 in the case of Thadou. The percentage of the majority of the tribal languages cannot be calculated as the census for these languages which are below 10,000 are not available. But it is evident that some of the minority languages are spoken by a marginal number of speakers and their existence remains hardly recognised. Thus, out of 33 or more languages spoken in the state, almost half of them are spoken by less than 10,000 speakers. With the Union and the State government doing very little for the protection and promotion of these minority languages, they are virtually reduced to a state where they have to depend for everything ranging from education to mass media in the language of the dominant language(s) (Manipuri) or languages of wider communication—Hindi and English.

Manipur presents an alarming situation of language shift in progress with many smaller linguistic groups giving up their language in favour of more dominant languages. The languages which are more vulnerable to language shift are the old Kuki groups. It is interesting to note that in most instances the direction in which these languages shift is towards the other neighbouring language(s) who speak(s) more or less similar language(s), though in some instances the shift is towards Manipuri. The case of Purum is one notable example of such shift where the speakers are fast changing to Chothe which is very much similar and related to Purum.

For lack of attention from the linguistic community, many of these lesser known languages have not been studied nor documented. The oral traditions too are dying out fast in the absence of written documents. Due to socio-economic backwardness of the people, even their linguistic rights remained unaddressed. The existing social-political unrest in the state makes them more vulnerable because many of these linguistic groups often have to rely on other more dominant groups for their safety and social security. If the linguistic rights of these minority languages are not addressed soon, it is feared that, many of them will die out in near future in favour of Manipur or the more dominant Kuki or Naga languages. Before discussing the factors responsible for language shift among the minority languages in Manipur, let us familarised ourselves first with the general notion of language shift and language maintenance from the socio-linguistic perspective.

Both language maintenance and language shift are collective result of language choice. Language shift simply means that a community gives up their language completely in favour of another one. On the other hand, a community is said to maintain their language if they collectively decide to continue using the language or languages it has traditionally used (Fasold, 1984). In other words when a speech community begins to choose a new language in domains formerly reserved for the old one, it is a sign that language shift is in progress. On the other hand, if the members of the speech community are monolingual and are not collectively acquiring another language, then they are obviously maintaining their language pattern. But what prompt a community to give up their language or under what conditions language shift take place? Fasold has pointed out two conditions associated with language shift-societal bilingualism and migration. Whatever may be the cause, language shift generally tends to affect the small, low-status linguistic group who shift to the language of a larger, higher-status group, though few fascinating cases in which the more powerful group has assimilated linguistically to the people they control politically. Also, the conditions under which language shift take place differ from language to language and from the socio-economic condition of the community who speak the language. On the whole, the following factors can be attributed for language shift in Manipur.

4.4.1. Restrictive Domains of Language Used

The domain of language used is very important for language promotion and language maintenance. The higher the domains of language used are, the higher the chances for its promotion and maintenance are. The domains in which most of the tribal languages of Manipur are used is either restricted to homes or village community life and in most cases, it does not extend beyond. These languages are neither documented nor used in schools or in mass media such as radio, newspaper or magazine, etc. Bible too has not been written in these languages. With the rapid penetration of mass media like radio, television, film, press, etc., the speakers of minority languages have to depend on Manipuri or the languages of wider communication such as Hindi and English. The All India Radio stationed at Imphal transmits their programme mainly in Manipuri, and partly in the language of wider communication. Out of the total broadcast, only 25-30 minutes duration are allocated for major tribal languages, viz., Thadou, Paite, Hmar, Tangkhul, Kabui, and Mao and that too mostly songs. The tribal languages of Manipur virtually have no place in television and press, though, few languages such as Thadou and Paite run their own vernacular newspapers.

4.4.2. Negative Attitude towards Mother Tongue

Language attitude plays an important role for language maintenance and language shift in a multi-lingual society. As is the case in most of the threatened languages of the world, in Manipur too, the community's negative attitude towards their language has further aggravated the problem of the minorities in preserving their linguistic identity. In the absence of any scope for the promotion of their language(s) in various domains such as education, mass media, etc., most of the lesser known languages mainly belonging the old Kuki group, viz., Chothe, Maring, Monsang, Tarao and Lamgang, etc., have started giving up their languages in favour of Manipuri and other neighbouring languages to a considerable extent, thereby limiting their language used only in homes or in village level only. The younger children in such circumstances are often swayed away by the language (s) of their peer groups. When a language has reached such a stage, a speaker of the minority language volitionally and conveniently identifies himself/herself with the language(s) of majority group.

Contrary to the case of the old Kuki group where the language shift is towards Manipuri or other dominant neighbouring languages, the case of Gangte and Simte (New Kukis) is somewhat different. Here, the language shift is towards the closely related language, such as Thadou or Paite. During my fieldwork in these areas, a Gangte lady who lives in Lamka town told me that, "we don't use Gangte in our home, my children speak either Thadou or Paite among their peers and we speak in Thadou with our children." Except in some villages where speakers of Gangte or Simte live in compact area, most Gangtes and Simtes have given up their language especially in regions where they live side by side with the Thadous or Paites. It should be noted here that, most Gangte and Simte speakers in Assam and Nagaland are totally assimilated to Thadou. In comparison to the Gangte and Simte, the Vaipheis are comparatively larger and are mainly found in Churachandpur district, hence, they are found to maintain their dialect though they are equally competent in Thadou and Paite. In sharp contrast to the rest, the Paites are faithful and loyal towards their language. The Paite's positive attitude towards their language has put them in loggerhead with the Thadous who constitutes the largest group among the Kuki-Chin group in Manipur.

4.4.3. Lack of Policy and Support from the Government

One of the most important factors responsible for language shift among the speakers of minority languages in Manipur is lack of support from the state government. In the absence any substantial support and encouragement from the government, the minority languages mostly belonging to the Old Kuki groups, viz., Purum, Chothe, Lamkang and Maring, etc., literally have no written literatures and are not taught even in schools. Thus, support and encouragement from the government will be of considerable help for the promotion and preservation of their language(s).

4.4.4. The Problem of Buffer Factor

Another factor which is responsible for language shift among the old Kuki-Chin groups in Manipur is "the problem of buffer factor" which from time to time plays the role of bridge communities. It should be noted here that, in the process of trying to bridge the two communities, i.e., the Kuki and the Naga, their languages too, are threatened in the process. Thus, the problem of buffer factor is one of the determining factors for language shift among the old Kuki groups in Manipur.

4.4.5. Measures to Prevent Language Shift

1. In order to prevent language shift among the minority languages, firstly the languages under consideration should be documented and grammars, dictionaries, pictorial glossaries, literatures should be produced. Translation of Bibles and Hymn books will be very helpful in preventing them from further shift.
2. The languages should be used in mass media such as radio, television, newspapers, and other magazines.
3. Above all, language awareness programmes should be organized from time to time to educate the people about their linguistic rights.

4.5. PROFILE OF THE LANGUAGES OF MANIPUR

This profile contains certain kinds of information for the languages of Manipur pertaining to geographical location, alternate name, dialect, classification, population, language use, and language development. Alternate names are given primarily for those languages having more than one name. Dialect names are given where they are needed to distinguish two forms of language. Attempt is made to provide the geographical location at various levels such as village, subdivision, and district in which they are spoken. The population statistic for each language is drawn from Census of India (2001). However, for those languages for which the census figures are not available in the Census of India (2001), they are taken from, Manipur State Primary Census Abstract for Scheduled Tribe–2001 and also from the Ethnologue.

Meitei/Manipuri

Geographical Location: The Manipuri speakers are distributed in mainly in Manipur, Cachar and Karimganj districts of Assam, West and North districts of Tripura. The speakers of the language are also found in the neighbouring countries of Bangladesh and Myanmar.

Population: 14,66,705 (Census of India, 2001).

Alternate Names: Meithei, Meiteilon, Meiteiron.

Dialects: Andro, Phayeng, Sekmay, and Khakching (C. Yashwanta Singh, 1995). Besides, it is the language of Pangal (Manipuri Muslim).

Classification: Manipuri is often regarded as constituting a genetic subgroup within the so called of Kuki-Chin-Naga group. But Burling & Thurgood (2003) pointed out that, there is no clear evidence to show that these subgroups constitute a larger super group though Manipuri shares some lexical similarities with the Kuki-Chin languages and Tangkhul due to prolonged contact between these languages. The position of Manipuri within the Tibeto-Burman is yet to be properly determined.

Language use: It is the official language of Manipur. The speakers of Manipuri also use English, Hindi and Bengali.

Language development: It should be noted here that Meitei Mayek was used until the eighteenth century before it was replaced by the Bengali script. Recently, the Meitei Mayek was reintroduced again as the writing system of the Manipuris (see Manipur Gazette 1980 for the approval of Meitei Mayek).

Grammatical Description: A fairly good numbers of grammatical descriptions have been done on the language. Some of which are listed below:

(1) Damant, G.H. 1875. *Notes on Manipuri Grammar.*

(2) Primrose, Arthur John. 1887. *Manipuri Grammar.*

(3) Primrose, Arthur John. 1888. *A Manipuri Grammar, Vocabulary, and Phrase Book.*

(4) Hodson, Thomas Callan. 1908. *The Meitheis.*

(5) Pettigrew, William. 1912. *Manipuri (Meitei) Grammar.*

(6) Robert, Shafer. 1961. *Native Names of Some Birds and Plants in Manipur, India.*

(7) Robert, Shafer. 1966. *Some Manipuri Words from Archaic Kukish Dialects.*

(8) Ningthoukhongjam, Khelchandra Singh. (1964). *Manipuri to Manipuri & English Dictionary.*

(9) Inder Singh. 1975. *Manipuri Phonetic Reader.*

(10) Madhubala P. Devi. 1979. *Manipuri Grammar.* Unpublished Ph.D. dissertation.
(11) Purna, C Thoudam. 1980. *A Grammatical Sketch of Meiteiron.*
(12) Warlbam, Raghumani Singh. 1989. *The Kwatha Dialect of Meitei.*
(13) Shiro, Yabu. 1992. *The linguistic position of the Meitei language.*
(14) Bhat, D.N.S. and M.S. Ningomba. 1997. *Manipuri Grammar.*
(15) Shobhana L. Chelliah. 1997. *A Grammar of Meithei.*
(16) Shobhana L. Chelliah. 2003. *Meithei.*
(17) Chungkham Jashawanta. 2000. *Manipuri Grammar.*
(18) Amy Kim & Seung Kim. (2008). *Meitie (Manipuri) Speakers in Bangladesh: A Sociolinguistic Survey.*

Aimol

Geographical Location: The speakers of Aimol are mainly spoken in three districts of Manipur, viz., Chandel, Senapati and Churachandpur. Aimol Khullen, Unapal, Satu, Kumirei, Chingunghut, Aimol Tampak, Khodamphai, Ngairong, Chandonpokpi, Soibong (Khudengthabi) are located in Chandel district, Tuikhong in Senapati district and Kai-Aimol (near Loktak Lake) and Luichungbum in Churuchandpur district.

Population: 2,529 (Manipur Primary Census Abstract, 2001).

Dialects: Related to Chiru, Purum and reportedly intelligible to Koireng.

Classification: Old Kuki (Grierson, 1903, Thurgood, 2003).

Language Use: In homes and community village life. Most speakers are highly proficient in Meitei. The younger people use mostly Roman script while elderly people use Manipuri written in Bengali script.

Hymn Book: *Biakruo La. Chongthar Rabu.*

Anal

Geographical Location: Anal are distributed in Chakpikarong and Tengnoupal subdivisions of Chandel district and one or two villages in Myanmar (Burma).

Population: 23,191 (Census of India, 2001).

Alternate Names: The neighbouring Meitei refers to them as Anan, while many Anals prefer to be addressed as Pakan.

Dialects: Laizo, Mulsom. Closest to Lamgang.

Classification: Old Kuki (Grierson, 1903 & Thurgood, 2003).

Language Use: Speakers also use Meitei. Roman script is used by younger generation and Manipuri written in Bengali script by older generation.

Bible: Pedinna Hrin Ru Tuna Lla (New Testament with Psalm).

Hymn Book: Puruwng Piipana (with Tonic Solfa), *Zochara Hla* and *Anal Hla Hrin* (meant for informal church gathering).

Primer: Thimbol.

Chiru

Geographical Location: Chiru are distributed mainly in three districts of Manipur, viz., Tamenlong, Senapati and Churachandpur. Lamdangmei and Dolang are located in West Tamenglong district, Dolang Khonou/Khoirok, Chiru Nungsai, Kangchup, Thangzing, Sadu, Bungte and Uram are located in Senapati district and Charoi Khullen in Churachandpur district. The speakers of Chiru are also located in Vaithou in Thoubal district and one village near Jiribam near the Assam border.

Population: 5622 (Manipur Primary Census Abstract, 2001).

Alternate Names: Chhori.

Dialects: Closest to Kom.

Classification: Old Kuki (Grierson, 1903).

Language Use: Speakers have high proficiency in Meitei. Older people read Meitei in Bengali script while younger people read English in Roman script.

Hymn Book: Tiekna Lah.

Chothe

Geographical Location: At present, the Chothe are distributed in around 15 villages, namely, Khongkhang, Chandolpokpi, Lunghu, Lirungtabi, Zeonthlang, Ajouhu, Pumthapokpi, Laininghu, Chandrapoto, Tampokhu, Purumchumbang, Old Wangparal, New Wangparal, and Lungle in Chandel district; Lamlanghupi in Bishnupur District; reported in Nagaland and near Myanmar border. Historians describe the Chothe as Purums as they settled at a place called Purum in Chandel district.

Population: 2762 (Manipur Primary Census Abstract, 2001).

Alternate Names: Chothe, Chowte, Chawte.

Dialects: Closest to Tarao and Purum.

Classification: Old Kuki (Grierson, 1903, & Thurgood, 2003).

Language Use: Purest Chothe is spoken in Purum Khullen. The speakers use Roman and Bengali script.

Gangte

Geographical Location: The Gangte are mainly distributed in Churachandpur district of Manipur. Some of the important village names are Chengkonpang, Gangpimol, Khousabung, and Vantungbung etc. The speakers of the language are also found in Myanmar.

Population: 14,500 (Census of India, 2001).

Alternate Names: Gante or Rante.

Dialects: Related to Thado, Chin, Vaiphei, Paite, and Zou.

Classification: Northern Kuki-Chin (Thurgood, 2003).

Language Use: The speakers of the language use mostly Roman script.

Bible: Pathien Lehkhabu Thiengtho translated by Khaigin Gangte and published in 1991 by the Bible Society of India.

Hmar

Geographical Location: The speakers of Hmar are distributed mainly in Churachandpur district of Manipur, Mizoram and Cachar district of Assam.

Population: 83,404 (Census of India, 2001).

Alternate Names: Hamar, Mhar, Hmari.

Classification: Old Kuki (Gerierson, 1903 & Thurgood, 2003).

Language Use: Speakers also use Mizo, Assamese and Manipuri. They use Roman script as their writing system. Ethnic Hmar living in Mizoram speak Mizo as first language.

Bible: Pathien Thuthienghlim.

Hymn Books: Hla Tharbu and *Independent Hlarbu.*

Grammar: P.N. Baruah Dutta (1996) *Hmar Grammar.*

Dictionary: Rochunga, Pudaite (2008). English—Hmar Dictionary

Koireng

Geographical Location: At present the Koireng are found in eleven villages, viz., Utonglok, Sadu Koireng, Nurathal, Iril Mapal, Ekpan, Kamu Koireng, Longa Koireng, Awang Longa Koireng, Tarung of Saikul, the Kangpokpi subdivision of Senapati district, and Lampohal Koireng in Imphal district. Villages of the Kangpokpi subdivision are situated on the eastern slopes of the Koubru-Leimaton range and face the Imphal Valley from Maha Koireng to Ekpan. Other villages are located in North-East portion of Imphal Valley in the Sagolmang-Pukhao side of Saikul with Ramu Koireng situated in the South-Eastern ranges of the Nongmeijing hills.

Population: 1410 (Manipur Primary Census Abstract, 2001).

Alternate Names: Kwoireng, Koireng, Kolren, Koren.

Classification: Old Kuki (Grierson, 1903).

Language Use: Adults can read Meitei in Bengali script while younger speakers read English in Roman script.

Koirao/Thangal

Geographical Location: The Koirao inhabit the mountain ranges to the south of Mao and Maram.

Population: 2348 (Manipur Primary Census Abstract, 2001).

Alternate Names: Kolya, Khoirao, Mayang Khong. In official records they are referred to as Koirao but they prefer to be identified themselves as Thangal.

Classification: Naga-Bodo (Grierson, 1903), Zeme group (Burling, 2003).

Language Use: Speakers also use both Manipuri written in Bengali script and Roman Script.

Kom

Geographical Location: There are around twenty-two existing Kom villages inside Manipur. They are Sinam Kom, Theiyong Kom, Laikot Kom, Ichum Kom, Kom Keirap (Upper and Lower), Khoirengtak, Sagang, Luikhumbi, Lallumbung, Mantak, Tuiringkhaison, Samulamlan, Chinglanmei, Bungsalane, Thampilan, Malnphai, Lananphai, Ngairong, Mungrushi, Sambangyan, Tonsen, Tampak and

Khulen. Most of these languages are located in the districts of Churachandpur, Tamenglong and Senapati.

Population: 14,673 (Census of India, 2001).

Alternate Names: Kom Rem is a common nomenclature for Kom, Koireng, Aimol, Chiru, etc.

Dialects: Kolhreng. Kolhreng may be a separate language.

Classification: Old Kuki (Grierson, 1903 & Thurgood, 2003).

Language Use: Fluent in Meitei. The speakers of the language use Roman script. Kom has one dictionary known as the *Englo-Kom Dictionary*.

Bible: Pathen Ṭong Intheng.

Hymn Book: *Christain Hlather.*

Kharam

Geographical Location: The Kharams are primarily found in Senapati district of Manipur. Some of the major settlements of Kharam are Tuirenphai, Laikot, Karam, Loikot Phaijol, Purum Likli, Kharam, Thadoi, Tampak Kharam, New Keithel Manbi Kharam and Khuram Khulen.

Classification: Northern Kuki-chin (Lewis, 2009).

Population: 1,400 (Ethnologue, Lewis, 2009).

Lamgang

Geographical Location: At present the Lamgang are distributed in around twenty-four villages, viz., Thamlakpokpi, Lamgang Khunou, Kompe, Leipung Tampak, Lamkang Khungai, Lamkang Khunthak, Lamgang Khunkha, Angbrasu, Paraolon, Challong, Mantri Pantha, Phunchong, Betuk Sengkreng, Nungkang Ching, Leingan Ching, Kurnu Ching, Purum Pantha, Charang Ching Khunkha, Charang Ching Khunou, New Chayang, Charang Ching Khullen, Kana Challong, Angkheng Chayang, Keithelmanbi and Sektai Karong.

Population: 5894 (Manipur Primary Census Abstract, 2001).

Alternate Names: Lamgang, Hiroi-Lamgang, Lamkaang, Lamkang.

Dialects: Closest to Anal.

Classification: Old Kuki (Grierson, 1903) But Thounaojam & Chelliah (2007) places it under Northern Kuki-Chin group.

Language Use: Most of the speakers of the language understand Meitei and they use both Roman and Manipuri written in Bengali script.

Monsang

Geographical Location: The Monsang are mainly settled in five villages, viz., Liwachaning, Heibunglok, Liwa Sarei, Japhou, and Monsang Pantha. These are all roadside settlements, located within the Chandel subdivision of Chandel district.

Population: 2,130 (Manipur Primary Census Abstract, 2001).

Alternate Names: Moshang, Monshang, Mushang, Mawshang.

Dialects: Closest to Moyon and Anal.

Classification: Old Kuki (Grierson, 1903).

Language Use: Speakers also use Meitei, English, and Hindi. Majority of the speakers can read and write Meitei (Singh, 1998) and they also use Roman script.

Hymn Book: Thangpa Lha.

Moyon

Geographical Location: The Moyon are primarily settled in 14 villages, viz., Komlathabi, Penaching, Heigru Tampak, Mittong, Khongjom Khunkha, Moyon Khullen, Mankang, Lamrii, Naplun, Minou, Khuwring, Khongtong, and Khukthar. The first three villages are located in the foothills of Imphal valley. Except for Naplun, which is located in the neighbouring country, all the remaining villages are located in hills surrounding the Imphal valley.

Population: 2,970 (Manipur Primary Census Abstract, 2001).

Alternate Names: Moyon, Mayon, Mayol.

Dialects: Related to Monsang and Anal.

Classification: Old Kuki (Grierson, 1903).

Language Use: The speakers of the language can read, speak, and write Meitei quite fluently. They are also conversant with Monsang and Anal (Singh, 1998). The speakers of the language use both Bengali and Roman script.

Purum

Geographical Location: In 1931 the Purums were located in four independent villages having not more than 20 to 60 houses in each village, viz., Purum Khulen, Purum Tampak, Purum Changninglong, and Purum Chumbang. The name "Purum" might mean "hide from tiger", as Tarakchandra Das and John Shakespear have suggested. In 1935, an anthropologist T.C. Das conducted a fieldwork among the Purums and found that there are around 571 speakers of Purum. Four decades, according to 1971 census, later the population of Purum was not available. The Purums have become extinct or they might have merged with cognate tribe Chothe.

Population: 571 (Manipur Primary Census Abstract, 2001).

Alternate Names: Puram.

Dialects: Related to Chiru, Aimol, and Langrong.

Classification: Old Kuki (Grierson, 1903).

Scholarly Works: Das, Tarakchandra (1945), *The Purums*, Needham, Rodney (1958), *A Structural Analysis of Purum Society*.

Tarao

Geographical Location: The Tarao are mainly concentrated in four villages of Tengnoupal district, viz., Tarao Laimanai, Leishokching, Khuringmul and Haikakmul. The village Heikamul is the latest which is situated near Pallel.

Population: 870 (Ethnologue: 2005).

Alternate names: Tarao, Tarau, Taraotrong.

Dialects: Closest to Chothe.

Classification: Old Kuki (T.C. Hodson, 1908 & Jashwanta, 2002).

Language Use: Speakers use Meitei or English. Older people can read Meitei in Bengali script, while younger people prefer Roman script.

Grammar: Chungkham, Jashwanta Singh (2002). Tarao Grammar.

Paite

Geographical Location: The Paite are mainly spoken in Churachandpur district of Manipur. Some of the important villages are: New Lamka, Pearson, Bungmual, Khuga dam (Mata), Tuithapi and in the district subdivisions of Thanlon and Singat. The speakers are also found in Mizoram and in Chin Hills in Myanmar.

Population: 64,100 (Census of India, 2001).

Alternate Names: Paite, Tiddim-Chin in Myammar.

Dialects: Bukpi (Bukpui), Dapzal (Dapzar), Dim, Dimpi, Lamzang, Lousau, Saizang, Sihzang, Telzang (Teizang), Tuichiap. Related to Thado, Vaiphei, Gante, Chin, Tedim Chin, Zou, and Simte.

Classification: Northern Kuki-Chin (Grierson, 1903 & Thurgood, 2003).

Language Use: Speakers also use Mizo, Meitei.

Bible: Laisiang´Thukhun Lui leh Thukhun Thak Kigawm translated by Nengzachin and published by the Bible Society of India in 1971.

Grammar Dictionaries: T. Chinzam (1964) *English-Paite Dictionary,* H. Kamkhenthang (1972) *English-Paite Dictionary*, B.B. Kumar *et al.* (1975) *Hindi-Paite Dictionary*, V. Thanglian (1978) *Paite-English Vocabulary*, T.C. Tiankham (1948) *English-Paite-Manipuri Wordbook.*

Grammars: T. Chinzam (1989) *Paite Reader III*, H. Ginpu (1960) *School English Grammar I*, T. Gougin (1962) *English-Hindustani Paite Primer*, K. Gouzagin (1989) *Meitei pau Zilna laibu (Manipuri Learning book part I&II),* T. Gouzagin (1989) *Hindi Paite Anuvad I & II*, K.P. Guite (1983) *English Paite Self Taught*, Kaizasong Guite (1978) *School English Grammar II*, B.B. Kumar *et al.* (1977) *Paite (Tedim Chin) Hindi Self Teacher*, Sarat Chandra (2006) *Paite Grammar.*

Simte

Geographical Location: The Simte are mainly found in Churachandpur district of Manipur. Some of the important villages are: Mingjang, Tubuong, Simveng, New Bazar, Thanlon, Leikangpai, Zouthang, Shumtuk, Monjon, Pamjal, Sasinoujang, Tallian, Dumsao, Khungung, Lungthul, Singhat, Moijin, Maokot, Suangdai, Suangpuhmun.

Population: 10,225 (Census of India, 2001).

Dialects: Related to Thado, Paite, and Zou.

Classification: Northern Kuki-Chin group Thurgood, 2003.

Bible: Laisiamthou published in 1993.

Thadou

Geographical Location: The Thadou are distributed over all the hill districts of Manipur. Majority of them are found in Churachandpur district, Sadar Hills subdivision of Senapati district and Chandel district. The speakers of Thadou are also found in the neighbouring states of Nagaland, Assam, Tripura, Mizoram and Myanmar. Of all the Kuki-Chin languages, Thadou or Thadou-Kuki constitutes the largest group in Manipur.

Population: The total population of Thadou is 1,90,595 (Census of India, 2001). The population of other Thadou speakers who are recognised as Kuki according to Census of India (2001) is 52,873.

Classification: Northern Kuki-Chin group Grierson, 1903 & Bradley, 1997.

Grammars: T.C. Hudson (1906) *Thadou Grammar*, M.S. Thirumalai (1972) *Thadou Phonetic Reader* and Shree Krishan (1980) *Thadou Grammatical Sketch*.

Dictionaries: Boinu Hangsing (1972) *Thadou Kuki Dictionary*, T.S. Agou Singson (2001) *Thadou Kuki Suonmantam Dictionary* and Pauthang Haokip (2007) *Thadou-Kuki Word Book: A Classified Vocabulary*.

School Text-books: Thimthu Zaila and grammar book *Paogil zu*.

Bible: The gospel of John translated by Ngulhau Thomson in "Thadou-Kuki" in 1942. Later the complete version of the Bible in *Kuki Bible*, translated by Tongkhojang Lunkim was published by the Bible Society of India in 1971.

Hymn Books: *Lathah bu* and *Houbung la*.

Journals: Thinglhang Post (editor Thangboi Haokip); *Sumkon* (editor Thangtinlen Lhungdim); *Jingvalpa* (editor P. Robert Haokip) and *Chenna Gam* (editor Thongneo Khongsai), Cholha (editor Benny Khongsai) and *Manmasi* (editor Lenneo Haokip).

Vaiphei

Geographical Location: The Vaiphei are found mainly in Churachandpur district of Manipur. Some of the major villages are: Lingsiphai, Tangnom, Kangvai etc. They are also sparely distributed in other district of Manipur. In other districts of Manipur, where they are found to live along side with the Thadou, they are partially or completely assimilated with the Thadous.

Population: 39,673 (Census of India, 2001).

Alternate Names: Bhaipei, Vaipei, Veiphei.

Classification: Northern Kuki-Chin group.

Language Use: Mostly Roman script.

Bible: The gospel of John was translated into Vaiphei by Walkin R. Robert and published by the Bible Society of India in 1917. The New Testament with Psalms was translated Siaklam in 1957. Later the entire translation of the Bible was published in 1981 by the Trinitarian Bible Society in London.

Grammar: S. Tinlal Vaiphei (1990) *The Vaiphei Primer* and Henzagen (1996) *Vaiphei Grammar*.

Zou

Geographical Location: The Zou are mainly distributed in Singat Subdivision of Churachandpur district and Chandel district. Some of the villages of Zou in Churachandpur district are: Zouveng, Zou Colony, Kamdou Veng, Tuitengphai, etc.

Population: 20,857 (Census of India, 2001).

Classification: Northern Kuki-Chin.

Bible: The New Testament was translated into Zou by Semkhopau Samte. A revised New Testament called *Thuhun Tha leh Sam Labupi* (with Psalm) was published in 1981 by the Bible Society of India. The entire Bible in Zou called *Pasian Laisiengthou : Tulai Zo Haam a kilekhie* was published in the year 1983 by the Diocese of Imphal, Bishop's house, Imphal, Manipur. Later another version of the Bible was translated by Taithul with the approval of the Bible Society of India published in 1992. Zou has two hymn books called *Labupi* and *Lathabu*.

Dictionary: Phillip Thanglienmang (2006) *Zo Poetic Words, Metaphors and Similes Vol.I.*

Rongmei/Kabui

Geographical Location: The Rongmei are mainly concentrated in Tamenglong district and in an around the Imphal Valley of Manipur. The speakers of Rongmei are also found in Cachar district of Assam and Nagaland.

Classification: Naga-Bodo (Grierson, 1903), Zeme Group (Burling, 2003).

Population: 94,758 (Census of India, 2001).

Bible: Nthamei Bible translated in 1989.

Hymn Book: Hymdai Lu.

Dictionary: Fr. Francis T.J. (1992), *The First Anglo-Rongmei Dictionary.*

Liangmai

Geographical Location: The Liangmai are mainly concentrated in Tamenglong district of Manipur and in Nagaland. Some of the important villages of Liangmai in Temenglong district of Manipur are Namtiram, Phelong, Taningjan, Inen, Machenglong, Gaililong, and Makhuilongdi. In Senapati district they are found in Kalatombi area of Senapati district. In Nagaland they are found in Samjuiram, Jhaluke, Paren, Medzephima district of Kohima. In Assam they are found in Upper Barak Valley.

Population: 34,232 (Census of India, 2001).

Alternate Names: Kacha-Naga, Liyang, Liangmai, Lyengmai, Liangmei, Kwoirong.

Classification: Naga-Kuki subgroup (Grierson, 1903); Zene group (Burling, 2003).

Language Use: The speakers use Roman script. Liangmai is merged ethnically with the Zeme and Rongmei to form the Zeliang (or Zeliangrong) community.

Bible: Masan Bou.

Hymn Books: *Hiuna Khombo Lui* and *Luisan.*

Dictionary: Dee Abonmai, ed. (2006), *English-Liangmai Sentence Dictionary* and N. Lungkingbow (2000), *The Raringki Liyangmai Naga Campicamrakeng Millinial Dictionary.*

Zeme

Geographical Location: The Zeme are also found in Tamenglong district of Manipur, Nagaland and Cachar district of Assam. Some of the important villages of Zeme in Tamenglong district of Manipur are Tousem, Impa, Taguaram, and Mandeu, etc. In Nagaland the speakers of Zeme are found in Jhaluke, Paren, Yangkhullen (Zeram) Yangkhunou (Bakie), and Medzephima in Kohima district. The important villages of Zeme in North Cachar district of Assam are Lodiram and Laisang.

Population: 34,110 (Census of India, 2001).

Alternate Names: Arung, Empeo Empui, Jeme, Zemi, Kacha-Naga.

Dialects: Paren, Njauna.

Classification: Naga-Bodo (Grierson, 1903) Zeme group (Buriling, 2003).

Bible: Samdegai Karchibe.

Hymn Books: *Helew Kanchibe* and *Helew Karchibe.*

Dictionary: N.H. Pouhau and Hiaduing Newme (2008). *Teluichu* (*Anglo-Zeme Dictionary*).

Mao

Geographical Location: The Mao are mainly distributed to the extreme north of Senapati district of Manipur. The speakers are also found in Nagaland.

Population: The population of Mao is not available in Census of India, 2001.

Alternate Names: Mao, Sopvoma.

Dialects: Paomata. Breton says Paomata and Pome (alternate name for Poumei) are the same.

Classification: LSI, Vol 3, Part II classified the language as Sopvoma or Mao-Naga and grouped it under the Naga-Kuki sub-group of the Tibeto-Burman.

Language Use: Speakers also use Meitei, but write mostly in Roman script. The Mao Bible was translated in 2001.

Grammar: P.P. Giridhar (1994) *Mao Grammar.*

Poumai

Geographical Location: They are mainly distributed in Senapati district of Manipur and three villages in Nagaland with appropriate population of 6,000 or more. Some of the important villages are Purul, Oinam, Phuba. The hymn books in Poumai are Poula and Loubvii.

Population: 51,000 (Ethnologue, 2005).

Alternate Names: Poumei, Paumei, Pomai, and Pome. Poumai is close to Mao. Not the same as Puimei (Breton, 1997: 217).

Classification: Poumai which was part of Mao has been recognised as separate tribe in recent times. The language belongs to Kuki-Chin-Naga sub-group of the Tibeto-Burman family.

Language Use: The speakers use Roman script. New Testament was translated in 1992.

Maram

Geographical Location: They are distributed in around twenty-two villages along the National Highway-39 in Senapati district of Manipur. Some of the villages are: Tumuyon Khullen, Mayangkhang, Rajaimei, Lower Sangkhongmei, Rümlung, New Maram, Maram Khullen, Willong Khullen and Katumei.

Population: 37,340 (Census of India, 2001).

Alternate Name: Maram.

Dialects: Willong Circle, Maram Khullen Circle, T. Khullen, Ngatan.

Classification: Naga-Kuki sub-group (Grierson, 1903).

Language Use: Men are more bilingual in Meitei than women. Most of the young people can read and write in Roman script.

Bible: Bangpü Rasham (New Testament).

Hymn Book: *Tammatoilü.*

Grammar: *Kashang Samret Bung.*

Maring

Geographical Location: The Maring are concentrated in the mountainous regions along the northern border of Chandel district.

Population: 22,326 (Census of India, 2001).

Classification: Grierson, 1903 and Bradley, 1997 classify the language under the Naga-Kuki group.

Language Used: Bengali script is used by older people and Roman script by educated new generation. The New Testament of Maring was translated into Maring in 2001.

Tangkhul

Geographical Location: The Tangkhul are mainly concentrated in Ukhrul district of Manipur.

Population: 1,42,035 (Census of India, 2001).

Alternate Names: Tangkhul, Tangkhul, Luhuppa, Luppa.

Classification: Grierson (1903) calls the language as Luhupa or Luppa and grouped it under the Naga-Kuki subgroup. Burling (2003) on the other hand places it under Tangkhul group.

Dialects: David Mortensen (2003) divided the speech forms of Tangkhul into nine varieties as discuss below:

(1) Standard Tangkhul: This is used as a medium of worship by the Tangkhul Christains. It is also used in education, government and literary purposes. According to Mortensen, *"This speech is mutually intelligible with the speech of Ukhrul town, but differs from it in several respects...Standard Tangkhul is now accepted as the intra-tribal medium of communication by young and middle-aged Tangkhuls (although there are still older people who do not speak it) but it has not displaced the so-called "village dialects"—the highly local and diversified languages employed at a family and village level".*

(2) Ukhrul: This speech is spoken in Ukhrul town, the largest settlement in the Tangkhul area. According to Mortensen most scholars working on Tangkhul fail to differentiate between this variety and Tangkhul language used as a lingua franca.

(3) Kachai: This variety is spoken by the people of Kachai village (located in the west-central part of Ukhrul district bordering Senapati district), is quite distinct from standard Tangkhul or Ukhrul dialect. This speech variety is spoken by slightly more than 3000 individuals, living in Kachai village or near-by Kachai village.

(4) Phadâng: Based on the wordlist collected by McCulloch (1859) from Phadâng vaillage, Mortensen is of the opinion that, Phadâng is an intermediate between Ukhrul and Kachai. He however, contended that *"this is probably due in part to innovations that have occurred in the Kachai area"* since the collection of his data.

(5) Huishu: This variety is spoken in Huishu village located in the northeastern part of Ukhrul district bordering Burma. According to Mortensen this variety *"is far more innovative than standard Tangkhul, Kachai, or Phadâng in its phonology, morphology, and lexicon. However, it still shares many of the distinctive characteristics of Tangkhul languages"* such as Champhung, Northern and Central Tangkhul, Khangoi, and Southern Tangkhul.

(6) Champhung: According to Mortensen this variety "seems to share some characteristics with Kachai and Phadâng, but

these are likely the result of conservation in these three languages as of shared innovation. Champhung is notable in preserving PTk final **-l*.

(7) Northern and Central Tangkhul: These varieties show great resemblance to each other and to other varieties mentioned above. Again, these varieties also share certain amount of lexical similarities with Kuki-Chin languages.

(8) Khangoi: This variety *"seems to share only slightly more with the core Tangkhul group than Kamarupan languages generally and seems to share a good deal with the Kuki-Chin languages"*.

(9) Southern Tangkhul: Mortensen is of the opinion that, this variety which Brown calls Southern Tangkhul is clearly a Kuki-Chin language, and there is no basis for classifying it as Tangkhul except for its tribal identity of the speakers.

Language use: Tangkhul is taught up to class XII as subject of instruction. The language is also used in All India Radio stationed at Imphal. The language is also used in magazines and newspapers.

Christian writings: The Holy Bible of the Tangkhul is called *Kathara Tui* and hymn book is called *Khokharumpao*.

Grammatical writings:

(1) D.N.S. Bhat (1969). *Tangkhur-Naga Vocabulary.*
(2) James A. Mattisoff (1972). *Tangkhul Naga Comparative Tibeto-Burman*.
(3) T. Luikham (1974). Tangkhul (Wung) Dictionary.
(4) Willaiam, Pettigrew (1979). *Tangkhul-Naga Grammar and Dictionary*.
(5) S. Arokianathan (1980). *Tangkhul-Naga Phonetic Reader.*
(6) S. Arokianathan (1982). *Tangkhul Folk Literature.*
(7) S. Arokianathan (1987). *Tangkhul-Naga Grammar.*
(8) S. Arokianathan (1995). *Tangkhul-English Hindi Dictionary.*
(9) David, Mortensen (2003). *Comparative Tangkhul.*

4.6. SCHEDULED TRIBES POPULATION IN MANIPUR

The population of Manipur in 2001Census had been 21,66,788. Of this 7,41,141 were Scheduled Tribes which constitutes 34.2 per cent of the total population of the state. The state had registered 17.2 per cent decadal growth of its Scheduled Tribe population in 1991-2001. There was a total of twenty-nine (29) notified Scheduled Tribes in the state. Of the total Scheduled Tribes in Manipur, Thadou is the largest with 1.8 lakh population representing 24.6 per cent of the state's total ST population, followed by Tangkhul (19.7%), Kabui (11.1%), Paite (6.6%), Hmar (5.8%), Kacha Naga (5.7%), and Vaiphei (5.2%). Among other major tribes, Maring, Anal, Zou, Any Mizo (Lushai) tribes, Kom, and Simte are having percentages between 3.1 and the rest of the Scheduled Tribes are comparatively small in number having less than 10,000 population each. The population of the Scheduled Tribes of Manipur is given in Table 3 below.

Table 3: Population of Major STs, Census (Manipur State 2001)

Sl. No.	*Name of the Scheduled Tribe*	*Total Population*	*Proportion to the Total Tribe (%)*
1.	All Scheduled Tribes	7,41,141	100
2.	Thadou	1,82,594	24.6
3.	Tangkhul	1,46,075	19.7
4.	Kabui	82,386	11.1
5.	Paite	49,271	6.6
6.	Hmar	42,933	5.8
7.	Kacha Naga	42,013	5.7
8.	Vaiphei	38,267	5.2
9.	Maring	23,238	3.1
10.	Anal	21,242	2.9
11.	Zou	20,567	2.8
12.	Any Mizo (Lushai) tribes	15,164	2.0
13.	Kom	14,602	2.0
14.	Simte	11,065	1.5

Excludes figures of Paomata, Mao-Maram and Purul sub-divisions of Senapati district of Manipur in 2001 census.

Table 4: Growth of non-scheduled languages—1971, 1981, 1991, and 2001 Census of India (Manipur State 2001)

Language	*1971*	*1981*	*1991*	*2001*
Anal	6,592	11,074	12,156	23,191.
Gangte	6,033	++	13,695	14,500
Hmar	38,207	36,365	65,204	83,404
Kabui	50,814	52,113	68,925	94,758

(Contd.)

Table 4: *(Contd.)*

Language	*1971*	*1981*	*1991*	*2001*
Kom	+	10,062	13,548	14,673
Kuki	32,560	49,478	58,263	52,873
Liangmei	+	++	27,478	34,232
Lushai/Mizo	2,71,554	3,84,528	5,38,842	6,74,756
'Maram	+	++	10,144	37,340
Maring	+	11,663	15,268	22,326
Paite	27,157	32,607	49,237	64,100
Simte	+	++	+++	10,225
Tangkhul	58,167	79,887	1,01,841	1,42,035
Thadou	51,054	57,536	1,07,992	1,90,595
Vaiphei	12,209	15,618	26,185	39,673
Zeliang	+	++	35,079	61,547
Zemi	+	10,619	22,634	34,110
Zou	+	1,215	5,966	20,857

4.7. MOTHER TONGUE EDUCATION IN MANIPUR

4.7.1. Constitutional Provision

The Constitution of India not only provides a fundamental right to the linguistic minorities for the safeguard of their language and culture, but also endeavours to "establish and administer educational institutions of their own choice *vide* Articles 29 (i) and 30 (i)". The Constitution also provides "adequate facilities for instruction in the mother tongue to children belonging to linguistic minority groups" through the special directive under Articles 347, 350, 350A and 350B. The first Prime Minister of India Nehru was a fervent advocator of minority and tribal languages. Nehru felt that the constitutional safeguard for minority languages were not enough and felt that the government should not only encourage the tribal and minority languages but these also "must be given all possible support and the conditions in which they can flourish must be safeguarded. In their matter of languages there must be no compulsion whatever." (Speeches cited in Mahapatra, 1993:176).

Articles 29 and 30 provide the right to conserve their language and script and to establish and administer educational institution of their choice. Besides, Article 350 gives the minorities the right to submit a representation for redressal of any grievance in their own language. A few more safeguards under Articles 350a and 350b were guaranteed to the minorities after the States Reorganisation Act of 1956 to provide facilities of education in their mother tongue at the primary level. Also to supervise the implementation of these safeguards a Commissioner for Linguistic Minority was appointed.

In spite of all these statutory guarantees provided by the Constitution, the linguistic minorities continue to lag behind development pursuits of the nation. This is evident from the literary ratio among the tribal all over the country. There is something lacking in the way the existing language policy and the kind of language planning processes that we ascribed to, which alienated the linguistic minorities especially the non-scheduled languages. As a result of these system, a vehement protest of minority language groups in the North East in the 1950s erupted over the imposition of Assamiya, or language movements of the 1960 and 1972 launched by Assamiya, and Manipuri movement for promoting Manipuri at official level.

Owing to policy of indigenisation of language and homogenisation of culture, linguistic minority in every state are facing ever increasing difficulties in matter of education, employment and other affairs of day-to-day life. Further, with the effort to replace English by the regional languages the disadvantage of the minorities wi'l be further aggravated unless their interests are protected by statutory law of the government.

4.7.2. Problems of Mother Tongue Education in Manipur

Ever since Manipur attained her statehood in 1972, the state has often witnessed a tug-of-war among dozens of tribal languages *versus* the dominant Meiteilon. The existing language policy and the kind of language planning processes the state government ascribed to, has failed to fulfil the educational aspiration of the linguistic minorities in the state. This is evident from the language problem which has erupted from time to time.

The language problem in Manipur erupted in the early 1980s when the state government tried to introduce Meiteilon as a compulsory subject up to class X. Later, the problem was settled by keeping Meiteilon as an option for the tribal in lieu of additional English or state's recognized tribal languages.

The problem over majority *versus* minority languages erupted again with the insertion of Manipuri in the Eighth Schedule in 1992. Recently, UPSC tried to impose Manipuri language as a compulsory subject in Civil Service (mains) examination for the candidates from Manipur state. But this was prevented by Guwahati High Court interim order to exempt the tribals from writing Manipuri language.

The recent introduction of Meitei Mayek (Manipuri script) has created a lot of social unrest from various sections of people in the state. The immediate instance was the demand for the affiliation of all Naga dominated areas to be included under the Nagaland Board of Education, which has resulted in confrontation of the Naga Student Union and the Government of Manipur.

The existing educational system of Manipur has immensely failed to fulfil the linguistic aspiration of the minority languages in the state. The existing language policy of the state has alienated the linguistic minorities of their right to be taught in their mother tongue. Out of the 29 or more tribal languages spoken in the state only few languages, viz., Thadou, Tangkhul, Paite, Hmar, Mizo and Zou are taught in schools while majority of the tribal languages remain neglected. The system of teaching is also faulty in that, the language policy-makers instead of introducing them right from the primary level, introduced them from classes XI and X which is not helpful for the development of tribal languages. The way the syllabus for these languages are designed too, has no significant impact to the learners of the language as only one paper on mother tongue is taught to the learners.

The problems of mother tongue education in Manipur may be summarized in the following words:

- In the first place, the minority pupils have very little opportunity for education in their mother tongue. The tribal languages of Manipur without being introduced first in the primary level are being introduced in IX and X standard which created a lot of gap for mother tongue learners. The pupils opt for it simply to avoid the burden of learning Manipuri (in Bengali Script) which is difficult for the tribal students.
- The system of education does not lay down certain norms and guidelines under which the tribal languages should be taught in recognized schools of Manipur.
- Under the prevailing situation, only Tangkhul, Thadou, Paite, Hmar, and Lushei are introduced while majority of the tribal languages are not even introduced at the primary level.

- In pursuing the three language formula in education the tribal languages of Manipur have to bear greater burden than the majority (Manipuri) in that they have to learn four languages in place of three, i.e., English, Hindi, Manipuri and their mother tongue.
- To tackle the ongoing language tussle within the state, the education department of Manipur notified in 22nd March, 1977, that the medium of instruction in primary schools having 90 per cent of pupils on its rolls belonging to any of the tribes within the State of Manipur shall be the respective tribal language with effect from the current academic session, i.e.1977. This is not effective because in case of the medium of instruction being that of the languages of the 90 per cent constituent, and the 10 per cent constituent belonging to minority are compelled to go with the majority or are opted out of that social class-group under compelling situation.
- The inadequacy of qualified teachers and the dearth of text books are also the major problems of mother tongue education in Manipur. Under the prevailing condition, it has become a burden for the school authority especially in private schools where many students from different linguistic backgrounds study together. In the absence of any grant from the education department, the private schools find it difficult to arrange teachers required to teach all the language subjects.
- In matter of employment too, they enter into an unequal competition with the majority candidates whose mother tongue is Manipuri. The Manipuri candidates can write in their own language as Manipuri is recognised as one of the eighth scheduled languages at the time of recruitment. Naturally, the majority candidates whose language is Manipuri will have greater advantage over the tribal minorities.
- The problem of minority language and mother tongue education still remained unsolved despite sixty years of Independence. The minority of languages need to be carefully handled in a multi-lingual society such as Manipur. The approach of the government towards the tribal and minority languages also needs to be changed as the tribal and minority

languages are the fabric of India's pluralism. Nehru's attitude towards the tribal and minority languages needs to be implemented in its truest spirit. The often distorted and patch work solution aimed to content the linguistic outcry of the minority and tribal languages need to be addressed from the grassroots level. For this, all the tribal languages irrespective of their population and size should be encouraged and all necessary help should be provided for their growth. The manner in which the tribal languages are taught should be modified in such a way that they are taught right from the primary level and the syllabus too, be revised and more number of papers should be increased if a permanent solution to the ongoing language problem is to be solved.

5

Linguistic Situation of Kuki-Chin Languages in Manipur

5.0. INTRODUCTION

The socio-linguistic situation of the Kuki-Chin languages in Manipur is very interesting at the same time very complicated. Linguistically, it is very interesting because not only their dialects are mutually intelligible, but the names of their clans too are the same for most of the Kuki-Chin tribes. For example, the names of their clans such as Hangsing, Singson, Guite, Lhungdim or Tungdim, Chonthu etc. are the same for many of the Kuki-Chin tribes. Linguistically, it is very complicated because, in spite of their mutual intelligibility and cultural similarities, they are classified as separate languages.

The term Kuki, though not popularly accepted in Mizoram in favour of Mizo, was still the unifying force among the Kuki-Chin speakers in other parts of North-East India particularly in Manipur, Nagaland, Assam and Tripura till the 1920s. The various tribes within the Kuki group accepted that they belong to the same linguistic group and live together in peaceful harmony till the 1920s. Unfortunately, the unity which held them together under one linguistic roof was short lived as it fails to fulfil the linguistic aspiration of various groups. For various political and sociological reasons, the term Kuki which was used to embrace these linguistic groups for quite some time became unpopular in Manipur around 1920s. The feeling of being different slowly and steadily paved the way for the rejection of the term Kuki by the smaller groups. During this period of internal crisis among the Kukis, the old Kuki groups joined the Naga National Movement which was gaining momentum on the parallel side. Other

Kuki groups (except Thadou speakers) who are geographically distal from the Nagas organised a new nomenclature 'Zomi'. Thus, the term Kuki which was used to imply the entire Kuki-Chin group in Manipur underwent a semantic narrowing and came to mean the speakers of Thadou in some sense. The overall situation of the Kuki-Chin group in Manipur may be summarised below:

- One of the problems which plagued the Kuki-Chin group after independence was the quest for common nomenclature which can embrace them under one linguistic roof.
- Most of the smaller groups within the Kuki-Chin felt that the quest for independent recognition under the term "Kuki" was derogatory and feared that the dominant group, probably Thadous, would dominate them. Thus, the feeling of being different slowly and steadily paved way for the emergence of "Zomi tribes" which is the conglomeration of seven tribes (see section 5.1 for the list of tribes).
- Unlike, the case of Mizoram, where the Holy Bible was written in Duhlian dialect, the Christian Missionaries have not written a common standard Bible for the Kuki-Chin groups who speak mutually intelligible dialects. With the translation of the Bible in almost all the dialects of the Kuki-Chin, the Bible became their most valuable literature to assert their linguistic identity.
- Tribe Recognition Act, 1956 further contributed to the process of split among the Kuki-Chin groups in Manipur. Thus, under the Act, each community chose to go for a separate tribe. Thus, the feeling of separate language for separate tribe further divided the already divided Kuki-Chin group in Manipur.
- In Manipur, the group's rivalry among the Kuki-Chin groups from time to time has further exacerbated the already divided Kuki-Chin linguistic group.
- The struggle for place of language domain between Thadou and Paite to be the language of lingua-franca and for the same domain in mass media such as radio is very much visible. (Note that the proposed All India Radio programme at Churachandpur could not be implemented over the dispute of host language between the Thadous and Paites).

Today, language competition is taking place consciously or unconsciously and any social movement directed at promoting one's own dialect is perceived by other as a threat to their dialects. People speak more of their differences than their common language and culture. This has created a lot of misunderstandings in the study of these languages, because many scholars including linguists who, without proper understanding of these languages often classified them as belonging to separate languages simply on account of their legal recognition as separate tribes.

5.1. THE PROBLEMS OF UNIFICATION UNDER A SINGLE NAME (KUKI)

Following the rejection of the term by the smaller tribes, there were renewed attempts to bring back the past unity under the term Kuki. Many native scholars have written a number of books emphasizing on common origin with the aim to forging stronger tie among these communities. From the 1960s, there were a number of movements, ranging from political to the student level in this direction. They believed that the Kuki-Chin group in Manipur could be united under one umbrella only if an acceptable common nomenclature was found for the group. The movements for unification were not successful because many of the smaller tribes had already developed a feeling of dislike for the term Kuki. Following the attempted failure to be united under the term Kuki, a political organization called Zomi National Congress (ZNC) was formed in 1971 at Daizang, Manipur. The seven cognate tribes from Manipur state—Gangte, Hmar, Paite, Simte, Tedim-Chin, Vaiphei and Zou adopted the name "Zomi" at Pearsonmun, Churachandpur on June 26, 1993. This alternative movement for unification under the term "Zomi", though successful for quite some time, faced a similar rejection first from the Gangte who later came back to the Kuki fold. Other tribes such as Vaiphei and Zou are divided among themselves into those who are in favour of the term Zomi and those who are not. Today, most of the tribes having their own underground (militant) group, a situation of alliance and counter-alliance is taking place among the different militant groups. There is a speculation that a common platform for all the Kuki-Chin groups can be reached in near future. Only time can tell us about such possibilities.

5.2. OVERCOMING BARRIERS THROUGH LANGUAGE PLANNING

Often, such language conflicts have far reaching social and political impacts towards their unification process. Since the Kuki-Chin speakers constitute one of the largest linguistic groups within the Tibeto-Burman family under the Eastern Himalayan ranges, they can be linguistically empowered than they are today, if such linguistic impasses can be amicably resolved. For this, a common consortium should be built on the line of modern language planning whereby all these languages would find their respective places. This can be attained only when the development of one language does not hamper the development of the other. Every language planner should bear in mind that, by suppressing the minor languages they are threatening their own existence as well. Some of the strategies to arrest language hegemony are suggested below:

- The constant engaged in language politic over control of power should be addressed in a planned manner.
- The historical antagonism over language politics should be buried.
- Language should be developed in a healthy manner, i.e., the development of one language should be an asset for the development of other languages.
- By developing bi-lingual dictionaries, grammars, glossaries, primers, etc.
- By encouraging bi-lingual programmes in mass media, television, bi-lingual newspapers, etc.
- Through bi-lingual education.
- Through bi-lingual corpus planning, status planning, etc.
- Through bi-lingual, seminars, workshops and exhibitions.
- Through bi-cultural exchanges and extravaganza.

In order to prevent unhealthy competition over language politics among the Kuki-Chin group in Manipur, an ideal language planning which can best represent them needs to be chalked out. For this, the role of language planner and an appropriate step from the government and the community is called for to solve the impasses over language politics.

5.3. MULTILINGUALISM

As stated earlier, the Kuki-Chin languages of Manipur are mutually intelligible to each other. In Churachandpur district, where most of the Kuki-Chin languages, viz., Thadou, Paite, Simte, Gangte, Zou, and Vaiphei are represented, the intelligibility is found to a great extent. It is not surprising to see people communicating in their own dialect language without any problem. The writing systems for all the dialects too are the same, i.e., the Roman script. One important observation about the Kuki-Chin languages in Manipur is that there is no dominant language. The absence of a dominant language has made the situation all the more interesting in that all the dialects flourished and has provided a perfect example of multi-lingual platform for all the Kuki-Chin languages. The Kuki-Chin groups in Churachandpur live in close proximity as a result they are competent in all the dialects. Different speakers meet almost everyday in public places, such as schools, market place, churches and sport meets. On the whole some dialects are commonly used depending on the place, where it is spoken. The overall linguistic situation in Churachandpur can be described as follows:

Whenever two speakers belonging to different languages/dialects meet:

- Both may use their own dialects to express distance towards or even dislike to each other. This particularly happens if the parties in discourse had met for the first time and both had a sense of loyalty towards their own dialects, or may be that both the speakers are not fluent in each other's dialect.
- Both may speak in the dialect of their choice if both are known to each other for a period of long time.
- It is also context dependent in the sense that if a speaker is a stranger among one of the other groups, he/she will use the dialect of that community to show his/her solidarity with that group. To cite an instance, if a speaker of Gangte goes to a Zou village he will use Zou to show his/her solidarity with the group and *vice-versa*.
- The choice to use or not to use a particular dialect among the Kuki-Chin speakers in Churachandpur district is solely dependent on the speaker. For instance, New Lamka, the main

town of Churachandpur district is mainly dominated by the Paites. So Paite is widely used than any other dialects. If a Thadou or Vaiphei customer happens to go to the shop owned by a Paite he may talk to the shop owner either in his/her own dialect or he/she may use Paite, and the shopkeeper will reply in Paite or in the dialect of his customer. Similarly, if a Paite customer goes to the shop owned by Thadou in Tuibong bazar where the Thadou speakers are dominant, he may talk to the customer in Thadou or Paite, and the shopkeeper may reply in Thadou or Paite.

- *Code-Switching*: Code mixing and code switching is a common phenomenon in Churachandpur. It is not surprising to note that in the same locality more than two dialects are usually spoken and as people meet frequently, the same speaker may use two or more dialects as the case may be. It is often noticed that a speaker of Zou or Vaiphei switches over to Thadou or Paite or *vice versa* or mixes his/her dialect with the dialect of the person he is talking to. They do this all the time in the course of their conversation.
- *Between the Kuki-Chin speakers and Manipuris*: Though Manipuri is widely spoken in all parts of Manipur, it has not taken root in Churachandpur as they constitute a small proportion of the total population. Most Manipuris in Churachandpur understand one or two dialects of the Kuki-Chin. In Thingkhangphai village which is 5 kilometres away from the town, sizable population of the Meiteis live side by side with the Thadous. Communication among the young people is carried out by mixing both Manipuri and Thadou, whereas the elderly people communicate in Manipuri most of the time.
- *Between the Kuki-Chin speakers in Churachandpur districts and other parts of Manipur*: In other parts of Manipur, where the Kuki-Chin languages are spoken, the mutual intelligibility seems to be less. When a Kuki-Chin speaker from Churachandpur meets his fellow Kuki-Chin speaker from other parts of Manipur they usually communicate in their own dialect, but still it does not pose problem for communication to take place.

- In other parts of Manipur where the Kuki-Chin and Naga languages are spoken communication between the two groups is always carried out in Manipuri.
- Most of the educated youths are bilingual in English as well. But the use of English is confined to educational institution and office only. It is interesting to note that, no two Kuki-Chin speakers in Manipur will communicate in Manipuri even though they may belong to different districts of Manipur.
- In the present days, most of the Kuki-Chin speakers are bilingual in Mizo. It should be noted here that though, only sizable Mizo population is found to live in Churachandpur, they are able to assert their language among other Kuki-Chin group especially in Churachandpur.

5.4. ONE LANGUAGE TWO NAMES (THADOU AND KUKI CONTROVERSY)

The confusion of different names for the same language is not only problematic for identifying the languages of the North-East India, but it can also disturb the unity, integrity and identity of the community for whom, no acceptable recognized name of the language/tribe can be reached. The problem of this sort is of pertinent issue for a long time among the so-called Thadou speakers in Manipur and in the adjoining states of Nagaland and Assam. There are varied views among the community about the name of their language. But, one thing has been certain that the language in question has been recorded as Thadou when referring to the language in question right from earliest traces of the language, such as Lieut. R. Steward (1857) and the Linguistic Survey of India (1904). They were also referred to as Khongsai or Khongzai (along with all the Kuki-Chin tribes) by the Manipuris in Manipur while in the neighbouring states of Nagaland and Assam they were referred to as Kukis by the neighbouring tribes. My contention regarding the name of the language is that, the language in question has no definite name but they were simply referred to as Khongsai or Khongzai in Manipur, Kuki in Nagaland and Assam Chin in Maynmar and by Mizo or Lushais in Mizoram.

The dispute between Thadou and Kuki to be the recognized name of the language started after the State Reorganization Commission (1956) which provided space for the growth of many regional languages. The State Reorganization Commission which was constituted to provide adequate facilities for instruction in the mother tongue at the primary stage of education to children belonging to linguistic minority groups and to safeguard the interests of the linguistic minorities do not stand in the interests of many linguistic communities in the state of Manipur. Thus, the lure for constitutional provision divided many homogeneous linguistic groups in the state. The recognition of Thadou as the name of their language after the Presidential Order published in the Gazette of India, Part II, Section 1, dated August 13, 1960 was not acceptable to all sections of the community who speak the same language particularly the Lukim's clan who were not part of Thadou clan proper. The non-Thadou contended that, Thadou is just of the clans in the genealogy of their tribe and could not be used to embrace them all. Since then, the non-Thadous were in favour of changing the name of the language from Thadou to Kuki.

The controversy over Thadou and Kuki was first seen over the publication of the Holy Bible in Kuki in 1971 with Mr. T. Lukim as the main translator. The publication of the Bible in Kuki was strongly condemned by the Thadous. This can be seen by the stand taken by Mr. T. Lunneh chief of Motbung village, located on the National Highway-39 on the position of the Bible Society of India, Bangalore that published HOLY BIBLE IN KUKI as recorded by Thirumalai in the Journal "*Language in India*" vol. 5:9 September 2005, is reproduced below:

- Kuki is a foreign word, applied to several Kuki-Chin tribes. Kuki is not a tribe and it has no dialect of its own, rather it is a national name like the Naga and Mizo.
- Thadou is a recognized tribe whereas Kuki is not.
- The publications in the past, including those of the Bible Society called the language in question either as Thadou or as Thadou Kuki.
- Mr. T. Lunkim is a non-Thadou. Hence he wants to change the name of the language from Thadou to Kuki.
- In our places, Thadou dialect is used by some Kukis who are not Thadous, but why should it forfeit its identity just because it is spoken by some non-Thadous?

- The ill-guided policy of Mr. T. Lunkim has now compelled the Thadou Pao Literature Committee, India to seek the end of justice at the judicial court.
- There is every chance for physical clashes among the communities involved. However, in spite of his position against the use of the term Kuki as the name of the language in which the Bible has been translated, it may be noted that, Mr. Lunneh himself was one of the supporter of the use of the term Kuki for other political reasons.

Thirmualai also wrote on the contention of T. Lunkim in favour of Kuki as:

> "Mr. T. Lunkim is a pastor and has been engaged in the translation of the Bible for several years, almost since the beginning of sixties. He belongs to a small community called Lunkim. This community is not part of the Thadou clan proper. However, people of this community speak the language as the Thadous. Mr. Lunkim's contention always has been that, since several non-Thadou communities speak the same language, the language should have a common name and not any name of a particular tribe, the use of which would make one concludes that the language belongs to the Thadou only."

The attempt made by the non-Thadou to change the name of the language from Thadou to Kuki has created a lot of social unrests within the society, which even resulted in physical clash among the Thadous and non-Thadous in Karbi-Anglong district of Assam and in and around Haflong in Cachar district of Assam. Even within the same speakers, majority of the people held the view that Kuki has no language of its own and implies many tribes who speak different dialects of the Kuki-Chin group and are not in favour of taking the name Kuki exclusively for their own.

The attempt to change the name of the language/tribe from Thadou to Kuki caused more harm to the community than it was intended. Because not only the pro-Thadous were unhappy, other tribes who belong to the Kuki are also alienated from the Kuki. Thus, instead of changing the name from Thadou to Kuki it would have been better had an alternative name acceptable to all was found, so that other Kuki tribes would still remain intact under the generic term Kuki. In spite of the effort on the path of the non-Thadous to change its name in favour of Kuki, Thadou still remains to be used in all India Radio Imphal, Manipur, and some churches such as Thadou Baptist Association still retain the name Thadou. The immediate impact of such attempt on the part of the non-Thadous caused a spilt within the society into Thadous and non-Thadous. This is evident from all the censuses of India taken from 1961-2001 which witnessed two separate names—Thadou and Kuki for the same group of speakers.

5.5. CONSENSUS FOR CENSUS

Anyone who had some experienced working on the language under consideration would immediately agree that the speakers of the language in question identified themselves as either Thadou or Kuki. The Census of India, 1961-2001 too, gave two separate names, viz., Thadou and Kuki for the same speakers as they are identified and recognised differently in different states of the North-east India. The question that needs to be asked is which of these two names represent the language under consideration? To this, it should be mentioned here that, neither Thadou nor Kuki can best represent the language in question, because Thadou is just one of the clans in the genealogy of the tribe like Haokip or Kipgen, etc. and Kuki is a foreign word used as a generic term and applied to several non-Naga tribes. But, as if in inheritance of its privilege as the name used in the past literatures, Thadou happens to be the recognised name of the language after attaining President's Order.

Following the controversy between the Thadou and Kuki to be the name of the language, the Census of India 1961-2001, classified Thadou and Kuki as separate languages. This has often led to the misrepresentation of the exact figure of people who speak the same language. For many who are unfamiliar with the two terms, Thadou and Kuki, this will give them the wrong reading that Thadou and Kuki are two separate languages, when both speak one and the same language. The reason for the misrepresentation of Thadou and Kuki arises partly because of the inability on the part of the speakers to arrive at a consensus name for their language and partly because the language is recognised as Thadou in Manipur, while in Nagaland and Assam the same is recognised as Kuki. Under the prevailing system, the speakers of the language may give his/her language as Thadou or Kuki depending on his/her loyalty with the two names or a speaker may give the name of his/her language depending on the region he/she resides as stated above. Further, majority of the masses, feel that, both the terms 'Thadou and Kuki' are acceptable to them and do not differentiate the two. As a result, they give their census report according to name (i.e., Thadou or Kuki) as it suits them. Therefore, when nationwide census is carried out on the basis of the prevailing situation this kind of anomaly crops in. In order to overcome such anomaly in the representation of the language in the Census of India, the following points have been suggested:

- In order to overcome the misrepresentation of Thadou and Kuki in the Census of India it is proposed that, the census should give only one label for the language as 'Thadou-Kuki', Thadou (Kuki) or Kuki (Thadou). Or a proper explanation should be given about the use of the two names, i.e. Thadou and Kuki.
- An awareness programme should be conducted through, seminars, workshops and symposia to arrive at a consensus name for the language in question.
- All the literary texts should bear the same name, when referring to the language in question.
- Any step taken towards the development of the language, such as language planning, status planning and corpus planning should be uniform throughout the regions where the speakers reside.

6

Introducing Kuki-Chin People

6.0. INTRODUCTION

The speakers of Kuki-Chin languages are known by different generic names depending on the regions they are spoken. Grierson Linguistic Survey of India (1904) refers to the denomination Kuki-Chin as a purely conventional one, without proper name corresponding to all these tribes. Grierson divided the Kuki-Chin group into two sub-groups, the Meitheis and the various tribes which are known under the names of Kuki and Chin. Vumson used the term **'Zo'** in his book '*Zo History*' to refer to all the Kuki-Chin speakers in India, Burma and Bangladesh. Chin is popularly used to embrace all the Kuki-Chin speakers in Myanmar (Burma). In the Indian sides of Manipur, Nagaland, Assam, Tripura and Chittagong Hill tracts, the term 'Kuki' is used. In Mizoram, the term Lushai or Mizo is used. Other alternative names include Zomi, Laimi, Hallam or Fallam, etc. In the words of Vumson, the term Zomi is a designation used by Paite, a people whose men wore a hair knot at the back of their head. Laimi is used by the Lai in Haka areas, in Falam and in parts of Matupi. Though, other appellations such as Meithei-Chin is possible, the term Kuki-Chin is widely accepted among the linguists in all the classifications of these languages. Grierson is of the opinion that the term Kuki and Chin are synonymous and both are used for many of the hill tribes.

6.1. KUKI-CHIN

The Kuki-Chin cluster, called 'Kukish' proper by Shafer encompasses Mizo and related Kuki-Chin languages. Mizo is also known as Lushai.

The Kuki-Chin groups are called Kuki in Assam, whereas they collectively referred by Burmese as əjc 'Chin' pronounced as [kʰâŋ] in the Arakan and [cʰÊ] in Burmese. The Chin is further divided into the Northern and Southern groups by Bernot and Bernot (1958) and Khyang is a southern Chin. More traditionally, the Kuki-Chin languages are divided into Northern, Central and Southern Chin. The ethnonym zó or zô is used by the Northern Chin of Siyin according to Kundall (1891) and Naylor (1925) are relatable to the second element in the ethnonym. (əšw) is used by ashõ, a Southern Chin group. Bernard Houghton had related the latter term to the Lushais or Mizo form dzó 'the generic term for Lushai race, and speculated that 'if these words are identical the Lushais and Chins, must, at no distinct time had form one race' (1892: 58). Godon Luce maintained that the Mon-Khmer influence in the form of loans is evident in the Chin than in the Sak or Luish languages (1985: 84).

The term Kuki is probably an Assamese or Bengali term applied to the hill tribes such as Lusheis, Rangkhols, Thados, etc. who have been known at a comparatively early period. Thus, in the words of Grierson (1904):

> "....the word Kuki is more especially used to denote the various tribes which successively been driven from the Lushai and Chin Hills into the surrounding country to the north and west. The tribes which first emigrated from the Lushai land into Cachar, the Rangkhols and Betes with their offshoots, are generally distinguished as Old Kuki; while it has become customary to use the term New Kuki to denote the Thados, Jangshens, and their offshoots. These latter tribes have driven the so-called old Kukis out of the Lushai land, and were afterwards themselves driven out by the Lusheis."

The term Chin is a Burmese word used to denote the various hill tribes living in the country between Burma and dialectically pronounced as Khyang. However, the name is not used by the tribes themselves, who use the titles such as Zo or Yo and Shö (Grierson: 1904).

The word "Chin" has been misinterpreted in many social contexts. Because its modern pronunciation is similar to that of the Burmese word 'basket', some people assume that the Chin people are so-called because they are people who carry baskets. To some it might sound strange that the above incident was a result of a sound change in Burmese language. In the old Burmese initial khy- and khr- merged into ch- which is the modern form. As a result, the old Burmese words khyang (as in tu-nge-khyang 'friend') and khrang 'basket' have the same pronunciation in modern Burmese.

According to Carey and Tucker (1896: 3), the name Chin is said to be a Burmese corruption of the Chinese 'Jin', or 'Yen', meaning 'man'. This pattern of speculation is further pursued by native scholars such as Lian Sakhong (2000: 57) and H. Kamkhenthang (1988: 3). The speculation is that the word Chin is cognate to Chinese 'Jin' or 'Yen' which is no longer recognized by the Kuki-Chin people as their collective name in modern time. According to Prof. B. Kalgren, however, the Old Chinese form for 'Jin' or 'Yen' which could mean 'man' is *nian (Karlgreen, 1957).

6.1.1. Distribution of Kuki-Chin

The Kuki-Chin languages are spoken in the southern hills of Manipur together with the state of Mizoram further to the south-west Chin Hills across the border of Myanmar are all occupied by the speaker of Kuki-Chin. The Kuki-Chin speakers are also scattered from Tripura up to the Chittagong Hill Tracts of Bangladesh.Vumson named 'Zo' for all the Kuki-Chin people and 'Zoram' for the land which covers a contiguous area of about 60,000 sq. miles, including Mizoram, Manipur, Tripura, Assam, Chin state and the contiguous area of Burma and some areas of Chittagong hills in Bangladesh. However, the name 'Zo' is not accepted by the people.

The Linguistic Survey of India (1904) records the geographical distribution of the Kuki-Chin as

> "....the territory inhabited by the Kuki-Chin tribes extends from the Naga Hills in the North down into the Sandoway District of Burma in the South; from the Myitha river in the east, almost to the Bay of Bengal in the West. It is almost entirely filled up by hills and mountain ridges, separated by deep valleys. This mountainous region, from the Jaintia and Naga Hills in the north, is the home of the Kuki-Chin tribes. We find them, besides, in the valley of Manipur, and, in small settlements, in the Cachar plains and Sylhet."

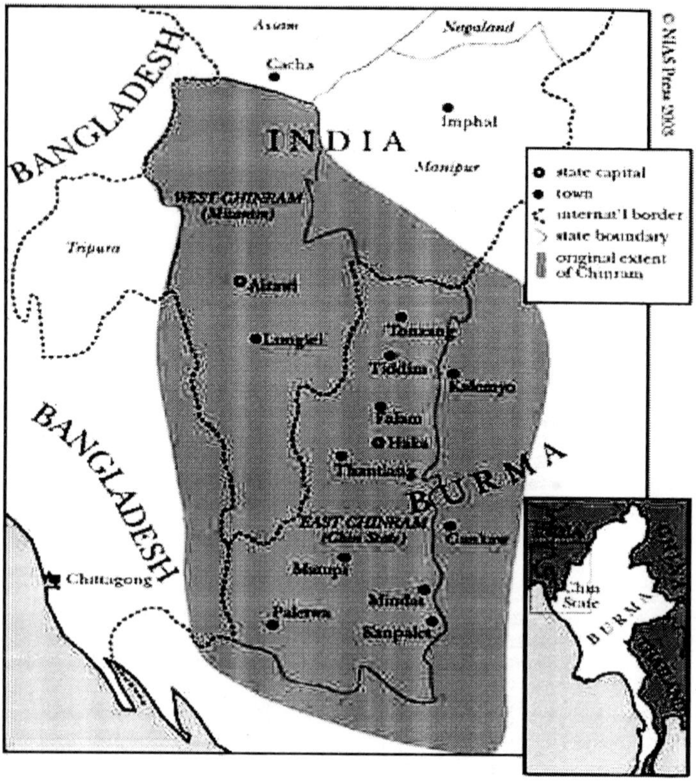

Fig. 9: Map showing the Distribution of Kuki-Chin Speakers

According to Shakespear (1912), the Kuki-Chin people are distributed over an area of about 25,000 sq. miles of the transborder region of Burma (now Myanmar), India and now part of Bangladesh.

In Manipur, majority of them are found in the districts of Churachandpur, Senapati, and Chandel, though they are also found in Tamenglong, Ukhrul, Imphal, Thoubal and Bishnupur districts as well.

6.1.2. Origin

The origin theory of the Kuki-Chin group runs in numbers. But most of the origin theories are based on myths and mythologies. One such mythological theory commonly held among the Kuki-Chin group is known as the **Khul theory**. According to their legend, it was believed that they originated from a cave called Khul or Chhinlung in their local dialects. In the absence of enough linguistic reconstructions and other archeological findings, it is very difficult to reconstruct the history of the Kuki-Chin. Scholars are also divided into two views; some believe that, the Kuki-Chin group originated in China through Tibet, while other believed that they came from Myanmar (Burma). The history of the Kuki-Chin tribes is only known from comparatively modern times. Grierson believed the settlement of Kuki-Chin tribes in Manipur valley for more than a thousand years. He is of the opinion, that they might have settled in the Lushei and the Chin Hills sometime during the last two centuries and this country may be considered as the place where their languages have developed their characteristics.

British sources record migration of Chin people westward from the Arakan across the Naf river into the Chittagong. Raids on neighbouring were not uncommon in the Indo-Burmese border lands, and 1770 Chin raid into the Chittagong which drew the attention of the British was probably just one of many episodes in a more general westward drift of populations in the wake of Burmese conquest of the central Burmese plains. At times when Burmese hegemony in the area made itself strongly felt by levies for the enrollment of troops and exacting of monetary tribute. The Chin people moved further westward to escape these heavy impositions, e.g., in 1596 after the fall of Pegu, in 1775 under king Alaungpaya, and again in 1784 after the conquest of the Arakan kingdom.

6.1.3. Population

The total population of the speakers of Kuki-Chin languages is quite difficult to estimate as they are distributed too widely under different sovereign states, viz., India, Myanmar (Burma) and Bangladesh. According to Vumson, there are about two and a half million Kuki-Chin speakers, half a million in Mizoram, 180,000 in Manipur, 50,000 in Tripura, Assam, Nagaland and Meghalaya, about 4,00,000 in Chin state of Burma, 3,00,000 in the plain of Burma, 50,000 in Somra tract and Hkamti or Naga district, 1,50,000 in Kale-Kabaw-Myitha valley and about 40,000 in the state of Arakan and 50,000 live in between the Sangut and Karnaphuli rivers of Bangladesh.

Grierson Linguistic Survey of India puts the figure of the Kuki-Chin between 6,00,000 and 10,00,000. In the absence of any reliable statistics available, most of the local returns were mere estimates. However, based on the information collected from the Linguistic Survey of India, the population of the Kuki-Chin is 6,00,000.

The figure of the Kuki-Chin according to the Linguistic Survey of India is shown in Table 5.

Table 5: Population Figure of Kuki-Chin (LSI, 1904)

Meithei		*2,40,637*
Northern Group		**60,345**
a. Thado	31,437	
b. Sokte	9,005	
c. Siyin	1,770	
d. Ralte	18,133	
		3,00,982
Central group		**1,07,604**
a. Tashon	39,215	
b. Lai	22,450	
c. Laskher	1,100	
d. Lushei	40,539	
e. Benjogi	500	
f. Pankhu	800	
Old Kuki		**48,814**
a. Rangkhol	7,820	
b. Bete	630	
c. Hallam	26,848	
d. Langrong	6,266 (?)	
e. Aimol	750 (?)	
f. Anal	750 (?)	
g. Chiru	750 (?)	
h. Hiroi-Lamgang	750 (?)	
i. Kolren	750 (?)	
j. Kom	750 (?)	
k. Purum	750 (?)	
l. Mhar	2,000	
m. Cchâ	?	
Southern Group		**1,10,225**
a. Chimme	?	
b. Weluang	?	
c. Chinbok	?	
d. Kindu	?	
e. Chinbon	?	
f. Khyang or Shö	95,599	
g. Khami	14,626	

6.1.4. Organisation of Village

Before, a village cite is chosen, a priest usually performs a ritual and blesses the village for the well-being of the people. A top of a ridges is preferably chosen, which can be easily defended from their enemy and also where they can fetch water using Bamboo flumes. Usually, the house is built in such a way that the entrance of the house faces, the East. They believe that rising of the sun is a sign of prosperity and good luck.

Traditional Kuki-Chin houses are rectangular in shape. It has a veranda type apartment where household articles are generally stored. The hen's cage is attached towards the lower portion of the veranda so that it can be protected from wild animals. The Kuki-Chin houses preferably have planks or spilt bamboo floor, where half of the house has an earthen floor meant for fireplace. The master's bed is adjacent to the fire place. The lower portion has an elevated apartment usually made of spilt Bamboo or planks for storing water and vegetables, it also has a window.

6.1.5. Agriculture

Agriculture is the main occupation of the Kuki-Chin people and their village economy too is totally dependent on it. The customs and traditions of the Kuki-Chin people revolve around the practice of shifting (Jhum) cultivation and are deeply rooted in the tribal lives. The lands are used for the maximum of two years of plantation and are left abundant for five to seven years so that the site is covered with enough trees which can be cleared for the next sowing. The villagers go to the forest and locate a site by cutting portion of the tree trunk or tie bunches of grasses in the border of their fields.

Before a cultivation site is selected the village priest performs certain ceremonies and the land is being blessed. If there are springs or rivulet, special ceremony is being conducted by the village priest to appease the wrath of gods of water within the site of the cleared land. The jungles are then cleared by hewing down trees. The cleared cultivation sites are kept for drying for at least a month before it is set on fire. The remnants of the fire are cleared and the land is tilt for sowing. The seed are usually sown during the first rainfall of the year. In case of paddy, the seed may be sown during monsoon. Weeding of the crops is done at least once before harvest.

The most commonly used tools used for cultivation are knife, axe, and spade. Most of the Kuki-Chin people observed certain ceremonies for different stages of cultivation. The first ceremony is observed just before the selection of cultivable land. The second ceremony is observed for good yielding after the crops have attained the nursery stages. The last and most important ceremony is conducted after the harvest as thanks giving ceremony for the good harvest. This event is observed by a community feast by killing a pig or cow and rice beer is being served.

6.1.6. Customs and Traditions

The emblem of the Kuki-Chin people is hornbill associated with their legend, faithfulness, fidelity and loyalty. The traditional Kuki-Chin people knot their head and were identified by their colourful shawls. Besides, they also celebrate different festivals which are based upon the cultural heritage of their communities. They have rich folklore and folk songs used for different occasions and purposes. The traditional Kuki-Chin people were fun-loving people and they enjoy amusing themselves by organising feast, festivals and sports from time to time. The Kuki-Chin people are also fond of songs right from their early tradition. Thus, wherever they move to new settlements they move along with their musical instruments such as flute, drums, guitars etc. They are also well-versed in making musical instruments even before the modern musical instruments were invented. This is evident from their folktales and folklores which were depicted in several immortal love stories. Till today the songs of the Kuki-Chin are well known among other tribes in Manipur. Kut is the common festival of all the Kuki-Chin groups and it falls on first November every year. In most of the Kuki-Chin tribal community, women occupy a lower status, and are not entitled to inherit parental property.

6.1.7. Religion

The traditional Kuki-Chin believed in supreme god called *pathen*, *pathian* or *pasian* in their local dialects to whom they sacrificed animals like dogs, pigs or hen as the village priest prescribed. They hailed him as almighty, omnipotent, omniscient and omnipresent. He is the giver of all good wishes of his people. They also believed in devils or demons. All sickness or bad fortunes are caused by such evil spirits. In order to appease such evil spirits, different types of sacrifices are offered by *thempu* (priest) to appease the wrath of the evil spirit. The traditional Kuki-Chin believed that, evil spirits reside in the lake, river and cave. The king of the evil spirit resides on the top of big mountain. They also believe that the devil spirit has great strength and can be transformed in the form of pigs, dogs or snakes. Sometimes, it appears in the form of shabby human being. Usually, when someone very dear dies in the family, selected strong man used to guard the graveyard of the dead with gun after the priest performed a ritual as the funeral graveyard. This is done, as they don't want the devil to take away the dead body of their dear ones. This continues for three to five days. In case an incurable disease has befallen a person, they blamed the evil spirit of the fields or village. In such case, the field or village have to be abandoned and sacrifices such as, red cock, mithun, pig or dog depending on the gravity of the sickness is scarified to appease the wrath of the evil spirit. The Kuki-Chin people also believe in life after death. Except in the case of unnatural death, a person can be reborn as another person.

6.1.8. Marriage

Traditional Kuki-Chin people follow the same system of marriage. With regards to selecting a bride, the Kuki-Chin tribes do not have a rigid system, except that the boy and the girl should not be closely related. When a boy attains a marriageable age, say 25-30 years, a suitable girl belonging to one's mother's brother's daughter is arranged on priority basis. But marriage with father's sister's daughter is not encouraged throughout the Kuki-Chin tribal communities. In case of failure to find a suitable girl from the mother's brother's daughter preference is given to girls belonging to mother's brother's clan. When a suitable girl is found, the boy's parent along with their relatives approach the girl's parent by offering traditional wine '*zu*' contained in earthen pot and suck through a bamboo pipe. While the wine is being served the negotiation starts. In most cases, the parents of a girl give the word for a second or even for the third round before giving their consent, but such invitation can be regarded as a positive sign. In case the parents of the girl rejected it in the first proposal, it means that the proposal is rejected once and for all. Once the negotiation is reached, the girl's parents negotiate for the bride price and time of the marriage is fixed. The bride price also differs from person to person and from community to community. Usually, a marriage girl gives up her clan's name and embraces the clan's name of her husband. Widow and widower marriage is also permissible throughout the Kuki-Chin communities. Monogamy is preferred by most of the Kuki-Chin communities. But polygamy is also prevalent as well. Divorce is also allowed, but when a husband seeks a divorce, he is required to report the matter to the village chief/village authority as the case may be and penalty is paid in the form of pig or rice beer. But when the wife seeks a divorce, she has to forego all that she brought from her parent's home at the time of marriage.

6.1.9. Birth

When a new baby is born, a priest performs certain rituals for the well-being of the new born child by sacrificing pigs or hens. The traditional Kuki-Chin communities believed that the name giving ceremony be performed as soon as possible, because they believed that the evil spirits might have a name of their own choice which might mean the death of the child. On the day of name giving ceremony, a priest sacrifices a fowl presented by the '*pu*', the brother of the child's mother and read omen from the movement of the legs of the dying fowl. The priest then ties a bundle of white feathers to the neck of the child and that of the mother with his blessings. Usually, the last syllable of grandfather or grandmother as the case may be is prefixed before the name of the new born child. This is a common naming system practiced by all the Kuki-Chin tribes.

6.1.10. Death

If someone dies in a village, his/her death is announced by ringing a bell or drum. Usually, the body of the dead person is washed and dressed in neat dresses. The Kuki-Chin bury the dead along with certain personal belongings. During the funeral, animals are sacrificed, cooked and shared by the mourners in remembrance of the deceased. The rich may slaughter several animals, but the poor ones at least with one animal. This is so done as they want to send their loved ones on the way to heaven with at least one animal. The meat is eaten in the home of the dead, and the remains are distributed among the relatives. The Kuki-Chin maintain two special burial grounds—one is used in case of natural death while the other is for deaths occurring unnaturally because of accident, epidemic, etc.

6.1.11. Hunting

The traditional Kuki-Chin people were renowned hunters and reputable warriors. In the event of successful big animal being killed, it is always associated by shouts of a slogan from the spot where the animal is killed up to the village. The nature of the slogan also varies from animal to animal. If the animal killed is a tiger, wild bawl, reindeer or elephant, the slogan is usually released while others are not released. Such slogans are only performed in case the animal is killed while hunting, while in the case of animals being trapped this is not performed. There are two types of hunting practices, one in which a forest is set on fire from below while the men with guns wait for the animals on the top of the hills where the animal are supposed to escape. This is usually done during winter when the entire forest is dry. The other type of hunting is carried out by beating drums and shouting slogans. In this type of hunting, fire is not used and this is usually done during summer when the forest is at the peak of its growth. In both the two forms of the hunting methods, male dogs are brought in the hunting field to chase the animals. Killing of elephant is considered as an attainment of one's masculinity. If a man kills hundred animals during his life time, it is celebrated as **sa-ai** which raises his social status. The event of **sa-ai,** is associated with a memorial ceremony in which bamboo of different sizes are erected in memory of the one who achieve **sa-ai** and the feast is celebrated with grand ceremony by killing mithun.

6.1.12. Foods and Drinks

Rice is the staple food of the Kuki-Chin people. Besides rice they also take maize, millet, peas, tapioca, sweet potato, and pumpkin.

They also grow fruit bearing trees such as orange, lemon, guava, citrus fruit, mango and banana. The Kuki-Chin people are also fond of non-vegetarian food such as beef, pork, mithun, chicken and flesh of many wild animals but majority of them abstain from buffalo meat although no restriction is imposed. They also like fish and go fishing regularly in nearby streams and rivers. Many of the Kuki-Chin people are also fond of dried fish. Eggs are not regularly taken. Green vegetables such as cabbage, mustard-leaf, beans, gourd, cucumber, melon, and yam grown in the field are consumed regularly. The Kuki-Chin people are fond of bees and honey. Usually, different types of bees are reared at home to obtain honey. They relish different forms of rice beer which occupy a prominent place in their social, ritual and cultural life. A very important food item, which the Kuki-Chin people would never miss is fermented meat or fish.

APPENDIX-I

The Comparative Vocabulary of Kuki-Chin Languages Spoken in Manipur

Symbols Used

Ņ = *Voiceless lateral fricative*
O = *Lower mid back vowel*
? = *Glottal stop*

Note: *The following six languages selected for comparative vocabulary are spoken in Churachandpur district of Manipur and show close lexical similarity.*

Nature

English	*Thadou*	*Vaiphei*	*Gangte*	*Paite*	*Simte*	*Zou*
air	hùi	hùi	hùi?	hùi?	hùi?	hùi
bank of river	lùipə′η	lùipə′η	lùipə′η	lùipə′η	lùipə′η	lùipə′η
brook	lùineo	lùiča	lùiča	lùita	lùineu	lùita
cave	kòhÓm	kòhÓm	kòhÓm	kòhÓm	kòhÓm	kòhÓm
cloud	méi	súm	méibuol	méipi	méi	méibuol
cyclone	čínpei	čínpei	čínpei	píηpei	píηpei	píηpei
desert	nèlgə′m	nèlgə′m	nèlgə′m	nèlgə′m	nèlgə′m	nèlgə′m
dew	dáitui	dáitui	dáitui	dáitui	dáitui	dáitui
earth	lèičúη	lèičúη	lèičúη	lèitúη	lèitúη	lèitúη

English	*Thadou*	*Vaiphei*	*Gangte*	*Paite*	*Simte*	*Zou*
earthquake	líŋ	linlíŋ	linlíŋ/lèilíŋ	zinlíŋ	zinlíŋ	zinlíŋ
echo	kit^{h}óŋ	kit^{h}Óŋ	kit^{h}Óŋ	kit^{h}Ón	kit^{h}Ón	kit^{h}Ón
fire	mèi	mèi	mèi	mèi	mèi	mèi
flame	mèikóŋ	mèikóŋ	mèikóŋ	mèikuaŋ	mèikuaŋ	mèikuoŋ
flood	túilen	túilen	túilen	tuilian	túilian	túilien
foam	∂p^{h}òn	∂p^{h}ùon	∂p^{h}òn	∂p^{h}ùon	∂p^{h}ùon	∂p^{h}ùon
ground	lèntol	léntól	léntól	léilak	tŭal	lèntual
heat	sa	sa	sa	sa	sa	sa
ice	bù?b∂′ŋ	vùk	vùk	vùk	vù?	vù?
lake	tuivei	dil	tuivei	dil	dil	tuivei
lighling	kólp^{h}é	kÓlp^{h}é	kÓlp^{h}é	k^{h}ólp^{h}éa	kÓlp^{h}ia	kÓlp^{h}é
mainland	g∂′mlai	g∂′mlai	g∂′mlai	g∂′mlai	g∂′mlai	g∂′mlai
marsh	dàm/ dàp	dÓpg∂′m	dÓpg∂′m	dÓpg∂′m	dÓpg∂′m	dàp
moon	Ṇà	t^{h}à	t^{h}àpi	xà	hàpi	hà /hàpi
moonlight	Ṇàva?	t^{h}àvàk	t^{h}àvàk	t^{h}àvàk	hàvà?	hàvà?
mud	bón	bón	bón	bŭan	bŭan	bŭon
night	zàn	zàn	zàn	zàn	zàn	zàn
outer layer of soil	lèiset	lèiset	lèiset	lèiset	lèiset	lèiset
rain	gò	gua	gò?	vua?	gua	guo
rainbow	Ṇàgúi	uizo	saxizouzum	saxituihup	saxituihùp	saxituihùp
rock	sóŋpi	sóŋpi	sŭoŋpi	sŭaŋpi	sŭaŋpi	sóŋpi
sand	nèldi	pieunèl	pieunèl	pieunèl	se?nèl	se?nèl
seashore	tùip∂′ŋ	tùip∂′ŋ	tùip∂′ŋ	tùip∂′ŋ	tùip∂′ŋ	tùip∂′ŋ
sky	vàn	vàn	vàn	vàn	vàn	vàn
stone	sóŋ	sóŋ	sóŋ	sóŋ	sóŋ	sóŋ
storm	hùipi	hùipi	hŭi?pi	hŭi?pi	hŭi?pi	hŭipi
sun	nísa	nísa	nísa	nísa	nísa	nísa

English	Thadou	Vaiphei	Gangte	Paite	Simte	Zou
water	tùi	tùi	tùi	tùi	tùi	tùi
whirlwind	čínpéi	čímpéi	číηpéi	píηpéi	čímpéi	píηpéi
winter	p^h∂`lbì	p^h∂`lbì	p^h∂`lbì	p^h∂`lbì	p^h∂`lbì	p^h∂`lbì
wood	t^{h}iη	t^{h}iη	t^{h}iη	t^{h}iη	t^{h}iη	t^{h}iη
world	xóvél	xóvél	xóvél	xóvél	xóvél	xóvél
Mankind, Sex and Kinship						
adopted child	mičakiva?	noučaga	miča kivak	taga?kivak	mitavak	tagakila?
ancestors	pu le pa	pu le pa	pu le pa	pu le pa	pu le pa	pu le pa
baby	nausen	nausen	nausen	nauηek	nauηek	nauηek
bachelor	golŅ∂'η	t∂'ηval	t∂'ηval	t∂'ηval	t∂'ηval	t∂'ηval
bride	móunu	móunu	móunu	móunu	móunu	móunu
bridegroom	móupa	móupa	móupa	móupa	móupa	móupa
brother-in-law	sopinuzipa	suapinu pas∂'l	suo?pi?nu pas∂'l	s∂'ηg∂'m nu pas∂'l	ma?pa	ma?pa
childhood	čap∂`nlai	naup∂`nlai	čap∂`nlai	naup∂'ηlai	naup∂'ηlai	naup∂'ηlai
co-wife	t^{h}aikem	t^{h}aikem	mei	mei	mei	mei/meinu
daughter-in-law	mounu	mounu	mounu	mounu	mounu	mounu/tapa zi
daughter-in-law's father	čapa zinupa	čapa azinu pa	čapazi apa	tapa zi a pa	tapa zi a pa	tapa zinu pa
daughter-in-law's mother	čapa zi anu	čapa ajinu nu	čapazi nu	tapazi nu	tapazi nu	tapazi nu
elopement	kizampi	kizampi	kitaipi?	kitaipi	kitaipi	zÒltai
father's brother (elder)	palien	palian	palien	papi	palien	palien/papi
father's brother (younger)	paneo	paneu	paneu	paneu	paneu	paneu

English	*Thadou*	*Vaiphei*	*Gangte*	*Paite*	*Simte*	*Zou*
father's sister (elder)	nilien	nilian	nilien	nilian	nilien	nilien
father's sister (younger)	nineo	nineu	nineu	nineu	nineu	nineu
father-in-law	te?pu	tekpu	tekpu	suŋpa	inte?pu	suŋpa
great-grand father	ipu apa	ipu apa	ipu apa	ipu apa	ipu apa	ipu apa
maternal aunt	nusopinumeihÒ	nu suapi numei	nu sua?pi? numei hÒ	nus∂′ŋg∂′ nu	nus∂′ŋg∂′m nute	nusuapi numei hÒ
mother's brother	pú	pú	pú	púnou	pú	pú
mother-in-law	te?pi	tekpi	tekpi	suŋnu	tekpi	suŋnu
nephew	sopipačapa	suapi pačapa	suopi?te čapa	s∂′ŋg∂′mpa tapa	s∂′ŋg∂′mpa tapa	s∂′ŋg∂′mpa tapa
niece	sopičanu	suapi tečanu	suo?pi?te čanu	s∂′ŋg∂′mpa tanu	s∂′ŋg∂′mpa tanu	s∂′ŋg∂′mpa tanù
paternal aunt	pasopi nùmei hÒ	pa suapi nùmei hÒ	pa suolpi? nùmei hÒ	pa suolpi? nùmei hÒ	pasuapi nùmei hÒ	pasuapi nùmei hÒ
paternal uncle	pasopipas∂l hÒ	pa suapi pas∂lte	pa suopi? pas∂l hÒ	pa s∂′ŋg∂′m numeite	pas∂′ŋg∂′m pas∂l	pa suapi pus∂l hÒ
sister-in-law	sopipazi	suapi pazi	suo?pi? pazi	s∂′ŋg∂′mpa zi	s∂′ng∂′mpa zi	s∂′ŋg∂′mpazi
son-in-law	tupa	čanu pas∂l	čanu pas∂l	tanupas∂l/ makpapa	tanupasa	tanupas∂l
widow	meit^{h}anu	meit^{h}anu	meit^{h}anu	meit^{h}anu	meit^{h}anu	meit^{h}anu
widower	pagÓŋ	pagÓŋpa	meit^{h}aipa	meit^{h}aipa	meit^{h}aipa	meigÓŋ
family	insuŋmi	insuŋmi	inkuon	suŋkuan	insuŋmi	inkuon
father	pa	pa	pa	pa	pa	pa
friend	lÓi	lÓi	lÓi	lÓi/lÒm	lÓi/lÒm	lÓi/lÒm

English	*Thadou*	*Vaiphei*	*Gangte*	*Paite*	*Simte*	*Zou*
husband	zipa	pus∂'l	pus∂'l	pus∂'l	pus∂'l	pus∂'l
mother	nú	nú	nú	nú	nú	nú
younger brother/sister	náO	náO	náO	náO	náO	náO
Fauna						
animal (domesticated)	insa	insa	insa	insa	Insa	insa
animal (wild)	g∂'msa	g∂'msa	g∂'msa	g∂'msa	g∂'msa	g∂'msa
animal	g∂'nča	g∂'n	g∂'n	g∂'n	g∂'n	g∂'n
ant	sikmi	sikmi/nì?sa	sikmi	sikmi	mi?si	mesi
bear	v∂'mpi	v∂'mpi	v∂'mpi	v∂'mpi	v∂'mpi	v∂'mpi
bedbug	m∂`t	xùmča	keiča	namsia	namsia?	names
bee	xói	xói	xói	xói	xói	xói
buffalo	lÓi	lÓi	lÓi	lÓi	lÓi	loi
butterfly	mitt^{h}a?	péηpelep	péηpelep	péηpalek	mitt^{h}at	mitt^{h}at
camel	saηan	saηÓηsau	saηÓηsau	saηÓηsau	saηÓηsau	saηÓηsau
cat	meηča	meηča	meηča	meη/zÓηeu	meη	meη
crab	ai	ái	ái	ái	ái	ai
crane	vakéηsáη	vakéηsáη	vakéηsáη	vakéηsáη	vakéηsáη	vakéηsáη
dog	ui	úi	úi	úi	úi	ui
dove	vaxú	vaxú	vaxú	vaxú	vapal	vaxú
duck	vatÓt	vatÓt	vatÓt	vatÓt	vatÓt	vatÓt
feather	vačamul	vačamul	vasamul	vasamul	vaha	vasamul
fish	ηá	ηá	ηá	ηá	ηá	ηá
fly	t^{h}òusi	t^{h}òusi	t^{h}òu	t^{h}òu	t^{h}òu	t^{h}òu
frog	ukéη	ukéη	ukéη	ukéη	ukéη	ukéη

English	*Thadou*	*Vaiphei*	*Gangte*	*Paite*	*Simte*	*Zou*
goat	kèlča	kèlča	kèlča	kèl	kèl	kèl
house lizard	daid∂`p	daid∂`p	daid∂`p	daid∂`p	daid∂`p	daid∂`p
insect	g∂'nhiŋ	g∂'nhiŋ	g∂'nhiŋ	g∂'nhiŋ	g∂'nhiŋ	g∂'nhiŋ
jackal/fox	sial	sial	sial	sial	sial	sial
leech	v∂`t	v∂`t	v∂`t	v∂`t	v∂`t	v∂`t
lion	humpiba?nei	sakeibaknei	sakeibaknei	humpinelkai	sakeibaknei	humpinelkai
louse	hit	hit	hik	hit	hit	hit
monkey	zóŋ	zóŋ	zóŋ	zóŋ	zóŋ	zóŋ
mosquito	t^{h}òukáŋ	t^{h}òukáŋ	t^{h}òukáŋ	t^{h}òukáŋ	t^{h}òukáŋ	t^{h}òukáŋ
nest	vačabu	vačabu	vačabu	vasabu	vasbu	vabu
owl	simbù	simbù	simbù	simbù	simbù	simbù
parrot	kipi	kipi	kipi	kipi	kipi	kipi
prawn	kaikóŋ	kaikóŋ	kaikóŋ	kaikuaŋ	kaikuaŋ	kaikuoŋ
python	gulpi/sam	gulpi	gulpi	gulpi	gulpi	gulpi
rat	zuča	zu	sazu	zu	zu	zu
sheep	kèlŋói	bèlàm	bèlàm	bèlàm	bèlàm	bèlàm
spider	maim∂'m	maim∂'m	maim∂'m	maim∂'m	maim∂'m	maim∂'m
tiger	kamkéi	kamkéi	kamkéi	kamkéi	kamkéi	kamkéi
tortoise	súmkóŋ	súmkuaŋ	súmkuoŋ	súmkuaŋ	súmkuaŋ	súmkuoŋ
vulture	mut^h∂'ŋ	mulukÓl	musane	valukÓl?	mulukÓl	musane/ mulukÓl
water leech	li:t	li:t	li:t	li:t	l:t	l:t
worm	lúŋ	lúŋ	lúŋ	lúŋ	lúŋ	lúŋ
yak	záŋsel	záŋsil	záŋsial	bÓŋtal	zaŋsial	zaŋsial
Flora						
apple	ep∂l	ep∂l	ep∂l	ep∂l	ep∂l	ep∂l
bamboo	gó	gua	go	gua	gua	guo

English	Thadou	Vaiphei	Gangte	Paite	Simte	Zou
banana	mÒt	na?čaη	na?čaη	na?taη	na?taη	nataη
banyan	móηp^{h}uη	móηkuη	móηkuη	móηkuη	móηkuη	móηkuη
branch	t^{h}iηba?	t^{h}iηbak	t^{h}iηbak	siηhiaη	siηba?	siηba?
brinjal	da?dil	m∂̑nta	da?dil	manta	vo?buol	vo?buol
cabbage	kopi	kÓpi	kuokpi	kuakpi	kuakpi	kopi
cane	tíη	tíη	tíη	číη	číη	číη
coconut	zubi	zubi	zubi	zubi	zubi	zubi
corn	min	min	min	min	min	min
cucumber	č∂'ηmai	č∂'ηmai	č∂'ηmai	t∂'ηmai	t∂'ηmai	t∂'ηmai
ginger	t^{h}í η	t^{h}í η	t^{h}í η	siη	siη	siη
grape	leηpit^{h}ei	leηpit^{h}ei	leηpit^{h}ei	leηga	leηga	leηga
guava	pumton/ kÓlt^{h}ei	kÓlt^{h}ei	kÓlt^{h}ei	kÓlt^{h}ei	kÓlt^{h}ei	kÓlt^{h}ei
lemon	č∂'mpara	č∂'mpara	č∂'mpara	č∂'mpara	č∂'mpara	č∂'mpara
maize/corn	kÓlbú	kÓlbú	váimim	váimim	váimim	váimim
mango	hái	hái	hái	hái	hái	hái
oak	g∂'ηpi	g∂'ηpi	g∂'ηpi	g∂'ηpi	g∂'ηpi	g∂'ηpi
pineapple	léηt^{h}ei	léηt^{h}ei	léηt^{h}ei	léηt^{h}ei	léηt^{h}ei	léηt^{h}ei
plant	t^{h}iηnóu	t^{h}iηnóu	t^{h}iηnóu	siηnóu	siηnóu/ haiči	siηnóu
pumpkin	mái	mái	mái	mái	mái	mái
root	zúη	zúη	zúη	zúη	zúη	zúη
seed	muči	t^{h}aiči	t^{h}aiči	haičitaη	haiči	haiči/muči
sugarcane	kÓlčú	kelzú	kÓlčú	kÓltú	kÓltú	kÓltú
sunflower	nisapa?	nisapak	nisapak	nisapak	nisapak	nisapa?
sweet potato	kÒkai	kÓlhá	kÓlhá	kÒkai	kÒkai	kÒkai
wheat	gèhu	gèhu	gèhu	gèhu	gèhu	gèhu
yam	bál	bál	bál	bál	bál	bál

English	Thadou	Vaiphei	Gangte	Paite	Simte	Zou
Body Parts, Bodily Conditions and Functions						
ankle	keηηoη/ axomit	keηηoη	siek	siak	sia?mit	sie?
belly	gilpi	gilpi	gilpi	gil	gilpi	gilpi
bone	gù	gù	gù?	gù?	gù?	gù
brain	Ņó?	tʰók	tʰuok	xuak	hua?	huo?
breast	nÓi	nÓi	nÓi	nÓi	nÓi	nÓi
tongue	léi	léi	léi	léi	léi	léi
cheek	bieη	bieη	bieη	biaη	biaη	bieη
chest	Óp	Óp	Óm	Óp	Óp	Óp
pace of the leg	k∂′l	k∂′l	k∂′l	k∂′l	k∂′l	k∂′l
deaf	naηÓη	bilηÓη	bilηÓη	bilηÓη	bilηÓη	bilηÓη
ear	bil	bil	bil	bil	bil	bil
elbow	kìu(čÓη)	kìu	tòη	tòη	kìu	kìu
face	mài	mài	mài	mài	mài	mài
penis	z∂′η	z∂′η	z∂′η	z∂′η	z∂′η	z∂′η
fever	xósi?	xósik	xósik	xósik	xósi?	xósi?
hair	s∂′m	s∂′m	s∂′m	s∂′m	s∂′m	s∂′m
hand	xùt	xùt	xùt	xùt	xùt	xùt
head	lú	lú	lú	lú	lú	lú
heart	lúηč∂′η	lúηč∂′η	lúηč∂′η	lúηt∂′η	lúηt∂′η	lúηt∂′η
illness	d∂′mlouna	d∂′mlouna	d∂′mlouna	d∂′mlou?na	d∂′mlouna	d∂′mlouna/ činatna
jaw	xà	xà	xàbe	xàbe	xà	xà
laugh	nùi	nùi	nùi	nùi	nùi	nùi
leg	kéη	kéη	kéη	kéη	kéη	kéη
liver	tʰin	tʰin	tʰin	tʰìn	tʰin	tʰin
lung	čop	čóp	čuap	tuap	tuap	tuap

English	Thadou	Vaiphei	Gangte	Paite	Simte	Zou
marrow	Ņin	t^{h}e?	čintuigu/t^{h}íeŋ	gu?ŋek	čintuigu?	čintuigu
medicine	d∂̑`mdoi/lóu	d∂̑`mdoi	d∂̑`mdoi	d∂̑`mdoi	d∂̑`mdoi	d∂̑`mdoi/ zatuizaha
mought	k∂̑'m	k∂̑'m	k∂̑'m	k∂̑'m	k∂̑'m	k∂̑'m
nail	tín	tín	tín	tín	tín	tín
navel	láimú	láimú	láimú	láimú	láimú	láimú
nose	ná?	nák	nák	nák	ná?	ná?
pregnant	gái	gái	gái	gái	gái	gái
saliva	tsíl	tsíl	tsíl	tsíl	tsíl	tsíl
skin	vùn	vùn	vùn	vùn	vùn	vùn
testicle	tílč∂̑'ŋ	tílč∂̑'ŋ	tílč∂̑'ŋ	tsílt∂̑'ŋ	tsílt∂̑'ŋ	tsílt∂̑'ŋ
thigh	m∂̑'l/ p^{h}èi	m∂̑'l/ p^{h}èi	m∂̑'l/ p^{h}èi	m∂̑'l/ p^{h}èi	m∂̑'l/ p^{h}èi	m∂̑'l/ p^{h}èi
throat	lÓl	lÓlŋÓŋ	gÓl	gÓl	gÓl	lÓl
tooth	há	há	há	há	há	há
urine	zùn	zùn	zùn	zùn	zùn	zùn
vein	t^{h}agúi	t^{h}agúi	t^{h}agúi	t^{h}agúi	t^{h}agúi	t^{h}agúi
vomit	ló?	ló?	ló?	lua?	ló	ló
waist	kÓŋ	kÓŋ	kÓŋ	kÓŋ	kÓŋ	kÓŋ
wing	Ņà	t^{h}à	t^{h}à	xà	hà	hà
Food, Drinks, Cooking and Utensils						
beef	bóŋsa	bóŋsa	bóŋsa	bóŋsa	bóŋsa	bóŋsa
chicken	á?sa	á?sa	á?sa	á?sa	á?sa	á?sa
chutney	m∂̑`lčame	m∂̑`lčame	m∂̑`lčame	m∂̑`ltame?	m∂̑`ltame	m∂̑`ltame
curry	mè	mè	mè	mè?	mè?	mè
dinner	niŅ∂̑'t ∂n	nitak ∂n	nitakn ∂n	nitak ∂n	nita? ∂n	nita? ∂n
honey	xoizú	xoizú	xuoizú	xuaizú	xuaizú	xuoizú

English	*Thadou*	*Vaiphei*	*Gangte*	*Paite*	*Simte*	*Zou*
lunch	sùn ∂n	sùn ∂n	sùn ∂n	sùn ∂n	sùn ∂n	sùn ∂n
mutton	kèlsa	kèlsa	kèlsa	kèlsa	kèlsa	kèlsa
pork	vò?sa	vòksa	vòksa	vòksa	vò?sa	vò?sa
soup	metúi	metúi	metúi	metúi	metúi	metúi
salt	či	či	či	či	či	či
tea	ča	t^{h}íŋpi	t^{h}íŋpi	síŋpi	síŋpi	nieŋtui/síŋpi
milk	bóŋnói	bóŋnói	bóŋnói	bóŋnói	bóŋnói	bóŋnói
liquor	zú	zú	zú	zú	zú	zú
Clothing, Ornaments and Care						
anklet	keŋŋÓŋO	keŋŋÓŋO	keŋÓŋxina	keŋŋÓŋO?	keŋŋÓŋO?	keŋ Óxi
bag	saxau	saxau	saxau	kÓl zaal	saxo	saxau/t^{h}u?pi
belt	kÓŋgà	kÓŋgà?	kÓŋgà?	kÓŋgà?	kÓŋgà	kÓŋgà
blanket	ponpi	zànpón /pón	puonpi	puanpi	puanpi	puonpi
button	ponkil	pónkil	puankil	puonkil?	puankil	puankil
cloth	pon	pón	paun	paun	paun	paon
comb	s∂'mt^{h}ì	s∂'mt^{h}ì	s∂'mt^{h}ì	s∂'msi?	s∂'msi?	s∂'msi
cotton	p∂`tčOn	p∂`tčOn	p∂`tčOn	p∂`tzam	p∂`t	p∂`t
frock	pon à?čoul	puanàkčual	puonàkčuol	puonàktual	puanà?tual	puanà?tual
lungi	ponvè	puanvè	puonve?	puanten	puanten	puonten
necklace	xi	xi	xi	xi	xi	Xi
ornament	kizèpna	kičèina	kizèpna	kizèpna	kizèpna	Kizèpna
ring	xùtzem	xùtsebi	zuŋbu?	zuŋbu?	zuŋbu?	zuŋbu
sandal	s∂nd∂l	s∂nd∂l	s∂nd∂l	s∂nd∂l	s∂nd∂l	s∂nd∂l
shawl	ponsil	pónsil	puonsil	puanza	puansil	puonsil
shirt	šÓŋxÒl	pónàk	puonàk	puanàk	puanà?	puonà?
shoes	kéŋkÒ?	kéŋtÒ	kéŋtÒ	xèd∂`p	kéŋkÒ?	kéŋd∂`p

English	Thadou	Vaiphei	Gangte	Paite	Simte	Zou
sock	mÒza	mÒza	mÒza	mÒza	mÒza	mÒza
umbrella	satin/váiph Ò?	váinilep	váinilep	váinilep	satin	satin
House, Part of House and Household Articles						
bed	zalxùn	lùpna	lùpna/pindan	lùpna	lùpna	lùpna
bedroom	lùpnaka	lùpna pind∂`n	kuolnaka	lùpna pind∂`n	lùpna pind∂`n	lùpna pind∂`n
box	t^{h}ilbÒm	t^{h}ilbÒm	t^{h}ilbÒm	siŋbÒm	siŋkÒŋ	silbÒm
bucket	b∂'ltin	b∂'ltin	b∂'ltin	b∂'ltin	b∂'ltin	b∂'ltin
chair	tòuna	čútna	čútna	čútna	tòuna	tòuna
cowshed	bÓŋbu?	bÓŋbu?	bÓŋin	bÓŋbùk	bÓŋbù?	bÓŋin
door	kÒt	kÒtxa?	kÒtxa?	kÒngxa?	kÒt	kÒt/kÒtxà
fireplace	t∂`pkòŋ	t∂`pkuoŋ	t∂`p/lùŋt^{h}u	t∂`ptùŋ	t∂`ptùŋ	t∂`pkuoŋ
knife	čém	čém	čém	tém	tém	tém
lock	čàbi	čàbi	čàbi	čàbi	čàbi	čàbi
mat	p^{h}é?	p^{h}ék	p^{h}ék	p^{h}ék	p^{h}é?	p^{h}é?
needle	hieu	pin	pin	p^{h}im	p^{h}im	p^{h}eu
pestle	sùk	sùk	sùk	sùk	sùk	sùk
rope	xáo	xáu	xáu	xáu	xáu	xáuhuol
shadow	le	le	le	le	le	le
thread	p∂`t	p∂`t	p∂`t	p∂`t/xauza?	p∂`t/xau	p∂`t
wall	báŋ	báŋ	báŋ	báŋ	báŋ	báŋ
well	tùikúl	tùikúl	tùikúl	tùikúl	tùikúl	tùikúl
window	kÒtča	tùkvel	kÒtča	tÒ?let	tÒ?let	kÒtta
basket	bÓm	bÓm	bÓm	bÓm	bÓm	bÓm
Farming and Agriculture						
agriculture	lóubol	lóut^{h}Óna	lóubÓl	lóubÓl	lóubÓl	lóubÓl
axe	héiča	héiča	héiča	héipi	héita	héi/heipi

English	*Thadou*	*Vaiphei*	*Gangte*	*Paite*	*Simte*	*Zou*
barn	čáŋp∂'η	bup∂'η	bu? in	bu?p∂'η	bu?p∂'η	bubu?/t∂'ηsal
breed	∂či	∂či	∂či	∂či	∂či	∂či
canal	tùilam	tùilam	tùilam	tùilam	tùilam	tùilam
chaff	čaηvái	busi	bu?si	bu?si	buvái	busi/taηvai
chaff remover	gudál	léidál	gódál	lÒ?pi	lÒ?pi	gódal
cutter	kÓite	kÓite	kÓite	kÓite	kÓite	kÓite
dam	túitinna	túitinna	túitinna	tùičinna	tùixÒlna	tùičinna
car	kar	kar	kar	kar	kar	kar
farmer	lóuŅoumi	lóut^{h}ómi	lóut^{h}omi	lóunasemmi	lóubÓltu	lóuhóumi
fence	thó	dái	dái	dái	dái	dái
fodder	g∂'n ∂n	g∂'n ∂n	g∂'n ∂n	g∂'n ∂n	g∂'n ∂n	g∂'n ∂n
garden	hò:n	hŭan	hŭon	hŭan	hŭan	hŭon
godown	vonkoina	vonkoina	vonxÓlna	vankoi?na	vonkoina	vonkoina
grain	čaηhúm	buhúm	bu?húm	∂nhúm	bu?t∂η	buhúm
gunnybag	borasaxáo	boradip	boradip	sai ipbag	boradip	boradip
handle	∂tu?na	∂tukna	∂tukna	∂letna	∂tukna	∂tu?na
harvest	čaηat	buat	bu?at	bu?at	buvua	bula?/buden
hay	čaηpÓl	pÓl	pÓl	bu?pol	pÓl	pÓl
husk	čáηvái	(čáη)vái	vái	vái	vái	táηvái
irrigation	tuipe?na	tuipiak na	tuipiak na	tuipekna	tuipiekna	tuila?na
land	gám	gám	gám	gám	gám	gám
manure	har/leihoi?na	har/leihoi?na	har/leihoi?na	har/leihoi?na	har/leihoi?na	har/leihoi?na
mill	čaηhe?naxÓl	xÓl	busuknaxÓl	∂nsuknaxÓl	xÓl	busu?na xÓl
nursery	∂ndÓnlai	budÓηlai	budÓηlai	bu?dÓηlai	bu?dÓηlai	bu?dÓnlai
pasture	h∂`mhíη	h∂`mhíη	h∂`mhíη	loupahíη	loupahíη	loupahíη
ploughing	lóukai	lóukai	lóukai	lóukai	lóukai	lóukai
spade	tùpe?	tùdál	tùdál	tùdál	tùdál	tùdál

English	*Thadou*	*Vaiphei*	*Gangte*	*Paite*	*Simte*	*Zou*
thresher	čeiroŋ	čeiroŋ	bu?suk	suk	bu?vo?na	busàtna
threshing	čáŋd∂'ŋ	buvó	buvÒ	∂nsu/bu?su	bu?vua	busat
threshing floor	p^{h}ól	p^{h}ól	p^{h}uol	p^{h}ual	bu?p^{h}ual	p^{h}uol/ busatnamun
weed	čaŋhám	bùhám	bùhám	bù?hám	bù?hám	bùhám
weeding	čaŋhàmbÒt	buhàmbÒt	buhàmbÒt	bu?hàmxóu	buhàmhóu	buhambÒt
Professions						
artist	lasami	lasami	lasami	lasami	lasami	lasami
drawing	limzit	limzi?	limzik	lemgel?	limgel	limgel
painter	limzitt^{h}iem	limzi?t^{h}iem	limziekt^{h}iem	lemgel?siam	limgelsiam	limgelsiem
author	laxazi?	lexabu zi? tu	le?xabu ziktu	laibugel?tu	laibugeltu	laibugieltu
beggar	xùtdÒ	xùtdÒ	xùtdÒ?	xùtdÒ?	xùtdÒ	xùtdÒ
barber	s∂'mhóu	s∂'mt∂'nmi	s∂'mt∂'ntu	s∂'mt∂'ntu	s∂'mmetu	s∂'mmet
scissors	ba?če	ba?če	ba?če?	sakolbakte?	ba?te	ba?te
blacksmith	t^{h}i?xéŋ	t^{h}isektmi	t^{h}isektmi	siksekmi	sikxéŋmi	siaxéŋ
butcher	sazó?mi	sazókmi	sazuokmi	sazuakmi	sazuaktu	sazuami
carpenter	t^{h}iŋt^{h}iem	t^{h}iŋnasemi	t^{h}iŋnasemmi	siŋsuisiamim	siŋsiammi	siŋlemsienmi
confectioner	mómóm zotmi	t^{h}ilt^{h}umzók	mómhúmzokmi	móamhumi zuakmi	čixumzuaktu	muomhúmzua
fisherman	ŋam∂nmi	ŋam∂nmi	ŋam∂nmi	ŋam∂mmi	ŋam∂mmi	ŋam∂mmi
gardener	honbÓlmi	hónbÓlmi	huonbÓlmi	huanbÓlmi	huonbÓltu	huonbÓltu
goldsmith	sanaxeŋmi	sanasékmi	sanaxénmi	sanasékmi	sanaxéŋtu	sanaxéŋmi
jeweller	xixéŋmi	xisiammi	xixéŋmi	xisékmi	xixéŋmi	xixéŋmi
grocer	mezó?mi	mezókmi	me?zuokmi	me?zuakmi	mezua?tu	mezuami
hawker	lexahÓmpa	lexahÓmpa	t^{h}ilhÓmmi	laihÓmmi	silhÓmi	silhÓmmi
hunter	g∂'mléŋmi	g∂'mléŋmi	sakapmi	sabéŋmi	sabéŋmi	sabéŋmi
postman	dakt^{h}a?pa	dakpu	dakpu	dakhÓmpa	dakpu	laihÓmmi

English	*Thadou*	*Vaiphei*	*Gangte*	*Paite*	*Simte*	*Zou*
potter	bélxéηmi	bélsekmi	bélxenmi	bélsekpa	bélsekpa	belxéηmi
shepherd	kelηoičiηpa	belamčiηpa	belamčiηmi	belamčiηpa	belamčiηpa	kelηuoičiηpa
Transport						
bullock cart	bÓηgari	bÓηgari	bÓηgari	bÓηléηkai	bÓηgari	bÓηgari
driver	garitol	garihékmi	garihékpa	garihéktu	garihéktu	garihékpa
harbour	kóηηa?na	lÓηηa?na	lÓηkiηaknamun	loηxÓlna	lÓηxÓlnamun	lÓηxÓlna
pilot	lenna hétpa	lÓηhékmi	lenna hékmi	lenna héktu	lenna hékpa	vanléηhék
reins	sakèinaxau	sahennaxau	sa kai?na xau	sakia?na xau	sakèina xau	sa kaina xau
rickshaw	riksÒ	riksÒ	riksÒ	riksÒ	riksÒ	riksÒ
sail	kitÒl	kitÒl	kitÒl	kitÒl	kitÒl	kitÒl
sailor	kòηtÒlmi	lÒηtÓlmi	lÒη tÓlmi	lÓηhekmi	lÒηtÓlmi	lÒηtÓlmi
ship	kóη	lÒη	lÒη	lÒη	lÒη	lÒη
train	relgari	relgari	relgari	relgari	relgari	relgari
wheel	garikeη	garikeη	garikeη	garipei	garipei	garikeη
Sense Perception						
acidity	∂t^{h}u?	∂t^{h}uk	∂t^{h}uk	∂t^{h}uk	∂t^{h}u?	∂t^{h}u?
bitter	∂xa	∂xa	∂xa	∂xa	∂xa	∂xa
black	∂v∂'m	∂v∂'m	∂v∂'m	∂v∂'m	∂v∂'m	∂v∂'m
blind	mitčÒ	mitčÒ	mitdù?	mitdel	mittÒ?	mittÒ
blue	∂dúm	∂dúm	∂dúm	∂dúm	∂dúm	∂dúm
bright	∂va?	∂vak	∂vak	∂vak	∂va?	∂va?
brown	zÓηrÓη	zÓηrÓη	zÓηrÓη	zÓηrÓη	zÓηrÓη	zÓηrÓη
coldness	∂d∂`pna	∂votdna	∂d∂`pna	∂votdna	∂d∂`pna	∂d∂`pna
deaf	naηÓη	béηηgÓη	béηηgÓη	bilηÓη	béηηgÓη	bilbiη
dumb	paut^{h}eilÒu	paut^{h}eilÒu	paut^{h}eilÒu	paut^{h}eilÒu	paut^{h}eilÒu	paut^{h}eilÒu

English	*Thadou*	*Vaiphei*	*Gangte*	*Paite*	*Simte*	*Zou*
fragrance	n∂`mtui	n∂`mtui	gimlim	gimn∂`mtui	gimtui	n∂`mtui
green	∂eη	∂eη	∂eη	∂eη	∂eη	∂eη
hot	∂sá	∂sá	∂sá	∂sá	∂sá	∂sá
red	∂s∂′n	∂s∂′n	∂s∂′n	∂s∂′n	∂s∂′n	∂s∂′n
sweet	∂úm	∂t^{h}úm	∂t^{h}úm	∂xúm	húm	húm
thirst	d∂′ηča?	d∂′ηčǎk	d∂′ηčak	d∂′ηtak	d∂′ηtak	d∂′ηta?
violet	ai eηrÓη	meixetrÓη	s∂′ndup	nÒtkuaη rÓη	s∂′ndup	s∂′ndup
affection	lúηsetna	lúηsiatna	he?pi?na	he?pi?na	hepina	ηaina
anger	lúηháη	lúηna	lúηna	hè?	hè?	luηt^{h}a?na
anxiety	luηd∂′η	lúηx∂mná	luηx∂mna/maksa	l∂′md∂′η	luηimna	luηx∂′mna
blame	ηÒ?	ηÒ?	ηÒ?	ηÒ?	ηÒ?	ηÒ?
Emotions, Temperamental, Moral and Aesthetic						
cowardice	mèis∂′n	dÒilÒk	dÒilÒk	dÒilÒk	mèidÒi	mèis∂′n
courage	háηs∂′n	háηs∂′n	háηs∂′n	háηs∂′n	háηs∂′n	háηs∂′n
doubt	ta?s∂′nlal	ginlel	giηla?	giηlal	ginmo?na	ginlana
envy	t^{h}aηse?	mitt^{h}ip	it^{h}ik	eη	t^{h}aηsietna	t^{h}aηsietna
grief	dana	dana	dana	dana	dana	dana
happiness	kipana	kipakna	kipakna	kipakna	kipakna	kipana
hatred	muda?	mùda	muda?	muda?	mudana	mudona/huotna
love	lúηsetna	lúηsiatna	lúηsietna	itna	lúηsietna	itna
pain	ná	ná	ná	ná	ná	ná
praise	pa?čà	pakčà	pakčà	paktà	pa?toina	phatna/ pahtÓina
pride	kiletsa?	kiletsak	kilitsak	kithupisak	kiliansa?	kiletsa?na
respect	zà	zàna	zà?	zàktak	zà?tat	zàna
sympathy	hepina	hepina	hepina	hekpi?na	hepina	hepina
terror	tizat	láu	láu	láu	záu	zaunapi

English	*Thadou*	*Vaiphei*	*Gangte*	*Paite*	*Simte*	*Zou*
weeping	kana	kana	kana	kana	kana	kana
wish	dèisa?	doidan	hihút	du?t^{h}us∂'m	dèisa?na	dèit^{h}u
wonder	l∂'md∂'η	l∂'md∂'η	l∂'md∂'η	l∂'md∂'η	l∂'md∂'η	l∂'md∂'η
Education						
book	lexabú	lexabú	le?xabú	laibú	lexabú	laibú
education	lexahetna	lexahetna	le?xahetna	siamsinna	siamsinna	siemzilna
illiterate	lexahelou	lexahelou	le?xahelou	lait^{h}eilou	let^{h}eilou	let^{h}eilou
ink	mùttúi	mùktúi	mùktúi	pentúi	pentúi	laitúi
library	lexakoina in	lexakoina in	laibukoina	laibukoina	laibukoina	laibukoina
map	g∂'mlin	g∂'mlin	g∂'mlin	g∂'mlin	g∂'mlin	g∂'mlin
notebook	boi	lexa puan	boi	laipuan	laigelna	laigelna lexapek
paper	lexapek	lexapek	le?xapek	laipek/le?xapek	lexapuan	lai/laipe?
pen	pen	pen	zikkai	laikuη	laikuη	laikuη
story	t^{h}usim	t^{h}ont^{h}u	t^{h}usim	taηt^{h}u	taηt^{h}u	taηt^{h}u
student	sùkul čap∂'η	sùkul naup∂'η	sùkul naup∂'η	sùkul naup∂'η	sùkul naup∂'η	sùkul naup∂'η
voice	Ógin	Ógin	Ógin	Ógin	Ógin	Ógin
Government						
vote	vót	vót	vót	vót	vót	vót
assembly	vaihopna inpi	kihouxÓmna	kisukxÓmna inpi	kixÓmxÓmna	vaihÓmna inpi	vaihÓmna inpi
boundary	g∂'mgi	g∂'mgi	g∂'mgi	g∂'mgi	g∂'mgi	g∂'mgi
city	xópi	xópi	xópi	xópi	xópi	xópi
country	g∂'m	g∂'m	g∂'m	g∂'m	g∂'m	g∂'m
freedom	zalenna	zalenna	zalenna	zalenna	zalenna	zalenna
glory	lòupina	lòupina/čoihoi	lòupina	t^{h}upina	lòupina	lòupina
government	sorkar	sorkar	sorkar	sorkal	kumpi	kumpi

English	*Thadou*	*Vaiphei*	*Gangte*	*Paite*	*Simte*	*Zou*
king	léηpa	léηpa	léηpa	kumpipa	léηpa	léηpa
kingdom	léηg∂'m	léηg∂'m	léηg∂'m	kumpigam/ lalg∂'m	léηg∂'m	léηg∂'m
queen	léηnu	léηnu	léηnu	kumpi nu	léηnu	léηnu
reign	vaihÓmlai	vaipuak lai	vaihÓmlai	vaihÓmlai	vaihÓmlai	vaihÓmlai
village	xó	xó	xó	xúa	xúo	xúo
War						
airforce	lenna sepei	lenna sepei	lenna sepai?	lenna sepai?	lennasepai	lenna galkap
army	gálsat sepei	sepai	leičuη sepai?	gálkapmi	sepia gálkap	gálkap
arrow	t^{h}∂'l č∂'η	t^{h}∂'l č∂'η	t^{h}∂'l č∂'η	t^{h}∂'lt∂'η	t^{h}∂'lt∂'η	t^{h}∂'lt∂'η
attack	bùłu	bùlu	bùlu?	suam/bùlu?	bùlu	bùlu
battle	gál	gál	gál	gálbÓl	gál	gál
battlefield	gáltol	gálmun	gáltol	gál mun	gálp^{h}uol	gálp^{h}uol
bomb	b∂̂m	b∂̂m	b∂̂m	b∂̂m	b∂̂m	b∂̂m
bow	t^{h}∂'l	t^{h}∂'l	t^{h}∂'l	t^{h}∂'l	t^{h}∂'l	t^{h}∂'l
bullet	mèič∂'η	mèič∂'η	mèič∂'η	t^{h}aut∂'η	t^{h}aut∂'η	t^{h}aut∂'η
ceasefire	hiem xám	hiem xám	hiem xám	hiamxám	hiamxám	hiemxám
enemy	gálmi	gálmi	gálmi	gálte	gálmi	gálmi
general	sepei lamkai	sepai houtu	sepai?lamkai	sepai? heutu	sepia lamkai	galkap maηpa
gun	mèit^{h}∂'l	mèit^{h}∂'l	mèit^{h}∂'l	t^{h}au	mèit^{h}∂'l	thau/meit^{h}∂'l
peace	č∂`mna	č∂`mna	č∂`mna	lèmna	lèmna	lèmna
sword	čemzám	čemzám	čemzám	namsau	temzám	temzám
treaty	kinùptona	kinùptona	kinùptona	kilemtua?na	kilemtua?na	kinùptona
victory	galzÒna	galzÒ	galzou	vualzou	galzÒna	galzÒna
war	gal	gal	gal	gal	gal	gal
armor	galv∂`n	galv∂`n	galv∂`n	galv∂`n	kithuamna	p^{h}o?

English	*Thadou*	*Vaiphei*	*Gangte*	*Paite*	*Simte*	*Zou*
crown	l∂'lluxu?	l∂'lluxu?	l∂'lluxu?	l∂'lluxu?	l∂'lluxu?	l∂'lluxu?
glove	xùttom	xùtóm/xùtbù	xùttom	xùttuam	xùttuam	xùttuom
gunpowder	mèilou	mèilou	mèilou	t^{h}avui	mèilou	t^{h}avui
villager	xómi	xómi	xómi	xómi	xómi	xómi
Law						
accused	ηÒ?	ηÒ?	ηÒ?	ηÒ?	ηÒ?	ηÒ?
adultery	azi aη a zoη	aηkÓm	aηkÓm	aηkÓm	aηkÓm	aηkÓm
bargain	dé?	dek	dek	dek	dé?	dé?
court	t^{h}ut∂'na in	t^{h}ut∂'na in	t^{h}ut∂'na in	kihekna in	t^{h}ut∂'na in	zum
debt	léiba	léibat	léiba	léiba	léiba	léibal
fine	leau	lieu	lieuna	liau	lieuna	lieuna
hanging	kixailit	xailùm	xailùm	kixailùm	xailùm	xailùm
judge	t^{h}ut∂'npa	t^{h}ut∂'ntu	t^{h}ut∂'ntu	t^{h}ut∂'nna bÓltu	t^{h}uxen	t^{h}uxen
judgement	t^{h}ut∂'nna	t^{h}ut∂'nna	t^{h}ut∂'nna	t^{h}ut∂'nna	t^{h}uxenna	t^{h}uxenna
language	pau	ham/pau	ham/pau	ham/pau	ham/pau	ham/pau
law	dàn	dàn	dàn	dàn	dàn	dàn
loyal	ginčatum	ginum	t^{h}u Ói	gin om	t^{h}udi?	ginum
murder	tolt^{h}∂ t	tualt^{h}∂ t	tualt^{h}∂ t	tualt^{h}∂ t	tuolt^{h}∂ t	tuolt^{h}a
oath	kitepna	kitiamna	kitiemna	kičiemna	kičiamna	kičiemna
protest	kip^{h}in	kip^{h}in	kip^{h}in	kip^{h}in/nialkal?	kip^{h}in	kiphin/nielna
rape	numei su?set	pÓηbÓtna	suol	sual/suam	suol	numei suol
reputation	mint^{h}∂`na	mint^{h}∂`na	hi?na	hi?na	mint^{h}∂`nna	mint^{h}∂`nna
suicide	∂ma le ∂ma kit^{h}∂t	∂ma le ∂ma kit^{h}∂t	∂ma?le? ∂ma? kit^{h}∂t	∂ma? le? ∂ma? kit^{h}∂t	∂ma le? ∂ma kit^{h}∂t	∂ma le ∂ma kit^{h}∂t
thief	guča	guča	guča	guta	guta	guta
victim	∂t^{h}ot tu	∂t^{h}uaktu	∂t^{h}uoktu	∂t^{h}uaktu	∂t^{h}ua?tu	∂t^{h}uo?tu
witness	sakhi	hetpitu	hetpihtu	theihpihtu	sakhi	sakhii/teči

English	Thadou	Vaiphei	Gangte	Paite	Simte	Zou
Religion						
altar	maičam	maičam	maičam	màitam	màitam	màitam
atheist	pat^{h}en ta?sanlou	pat^{h}ian giŋlou	pat^{h}ienÓiloumi	patian t^{h}u Óilou	patian giŋtalou	giŋloumi
bell	da?	dak	dak	dak	da?	da?
blessing	patheina	malsÓm	vaŋboukna	vualzOlna	vualzOlna	guolzOna
church	hou in	biak in	biak in	biak in	bia? in	bie? In
circumcision	čeptɘ̑n	čeptɘ̑n	čeptɘ̑n	zeksum	teptɘ̑n	teptɘ̑n
devil	diabol	diabɘl	diabol	dOi	dOi	dOi/ doimaŋpa
festival	kùmhei	kùmhei	gulnùp	nit^{h}upi	kut	pOi/kut
ghost	t^{h}iŅa	t^{h}it^{h}a	t^{h}it^{h}a	sixa	sixa	siha
heaven	vàngɘ′m	vàngɘ′m	vàngɘ′m	vàngɘ′m	vàngɘ′m	vàngɘ′m
hell	mèidil	mèidil	mèidiel	mèidil	mèidil	mèidil
Idol	milim	milim	milim	milim	milim	milim
offering	maičam	t^{h}o?lÒm	t^{h}o?lÒm	t^{h}o?lÒm	t^{h}o?lÒm	t^{h}o?lÒm
prayer	táona	páučɘ`p	páučɘ`m	t^{h}umna	t^{h}umna	t^{h}umna/ t^{h}uŋe?na
prophet/priest	t^{h}iemgaO	zÓlnei	thíempu	zÓlnei	síampu	síampu
sermon	t^{h}uhil	t^{h}uhil	t^{h}uhil	t^{h}ugen	t^{h}ugapi	t^{h}ugen
sin	čÓnset	gitlòuna	gitlòu?na	xel?na	xelna	xelna/mÒna
spirit	Ņagao	t^{h}agau	t^{h}agau	xa	hagau	hagau
worship together	houxÓm	houxÓm	houxÓm	biakna	houxÓm	bie?na
Games and Sports						
athlete	kičimmi	kehelmi	kičimmi	kimÒlmi	kičiemmi	kimÒlmi
game	kičip/golset	kehɘ`lna	guolsiek	kimÒlna	kimÒlna	kimÒlna
kite	lexaléŋ	lexaléŋ	lexaléŋ	lailéŋ	lailéŋ	lailéŋ / lexaléŋ
playingcards	Lexakàp	lexakàp	lexakàp	laikàp	laikàp	laikàp
race	kiŅeitet	kitaitet	kitai el	kitaitet	taikidamna	taikidamna
whistle	mùtgiŋ	mùtgiŋ/philip	mùtgì?	mùtgiŋ/p^{h}it	mùtgiŋ	mùtgiŋ

English	*Thadou*	*Vaiphei*	*Gangte*	*Paite*	*Simte*	*Zou*
Entertainment						
actor	limt^{h}Òpa	limt^{h}Òpa	lim t^{h}Ò? pa	lemčiŋpa	limčaŋpa	limčiŋpa
actress	limt^{h}Ònu	limt^{h}Ònu	limt^{h}Ònu	lemčiŋnu	limčaŋnu	limčiŋnu
dancer	∂lammi	∂lammi	∂lammi	∂lammi	∂lammi	∂lammi
drum	xoŋ	xóŋ	xuoŋ	xuaŋ	xuaŋ	xuoŋ
flute	t^{h}eile	t^{h}eile	čaŋŋai	tamŋai	t^{h}eile	t^{h}eile
singer	lasa mi	lasami	lasami	lasami	lasami	lasami
song	la	la	la	la	la	la
stage	dÒxáŋ	dÒkán	dÒxáŋ	dÒ?káŋ	dÒxáŋ	dÒxáŋ / dÒsáŋ
tone	Ógìn	Ógìt	Ógìn/ Ógì?	Ógìn	Ógìn	Ógìn
tune	lakei	lakai	la kai?	la kai?	lakai	lakai
Adjectives and Abstract Nouns						
all	∂bÓnnin	∂bÓnnin	∂bÓnnin	∂vekkin	∂bÓnnin	∂bÓnnin/ zousie
big	∂lien	∂lian	∂lien	∂lian	∂lien	∂lien
brave	haŋs∂'n	haŋs∂'n	haŋs∂'n	haŋs∂'n	haŋs∂'n	haŋs∂'n
charming	mum	mumhÒi	mum	melhÒi?	etlÒm	etlÒm
civilized	x∂'ŋtou	x∂'ŋtou	x∂'ŋtou/ č∂'ŋkaŋ	x∂'ŋtou	x∂'ŋtou/xotáŋpil	x∂'ŋtou/ xotaŋpil
clever	∂čiŋ/∂pil	∂čiŋ/∂pil	∂čiŋ/∂pil	∂pil	∂pil	∂pil
deep	∂t^{h}u?	∂t^{h}uk	∂t^{h}uk	∂t^{h}uk	∂t^{h}u?	∂t^{h}u?
emptiness	hÓmna	hÓmna/∂Óŋ	hÓmna/∂Óŋ	hÓmna	hÓmna	hÓmna
famous	mint^{h}aŋ	mint^{h}aŋ	mint^{h}aŋ	mint^{h}aŋ	mint^{h}aŋ	mint^{h}aŋ
fame	mìnt^{h}∂`nna	mìnt^{h}∂`nna	mìnt^{h}∂`nna	mìnt^{h}∂`nna	mìnt^{h}∂`nna	mìnt^{h}∂`nna
foolishness	ŋÒlna	ŋÒlna	ŋÒlna	haina	haina	motna
guilty	mÒč∂`n	mÒna	mÒ?na	mÒ?na	mÒna	mÒna
humorous	nuizatum	nuizatum	nuizatum	nui?zat^{h}uai	nuizatt^{h}u	nuizat^{h}uoi

English	Thadou	Vaiphei	Gangte	Paite	Simte	Zou
kindness	p^{h}∂`tna	p^{h}∂`tna	p^{h}∂`tna	p^{h}∂`tna	p^{h}∂`tna	p^{h}∂`tna
naughty	∂xel	∂xel	∂xel	∂xel/ÓmmÓ?	∂xel	∂xel
mad	∂ηÓl	∂ηÓl	∂ηÓl	∂hai	∂hai	∂mÒ
richness	housatna	hausakna	hausakna	hau?sakna	hausatna	hausatna
smallness	neuna	neuna	neuna	neuna	neuna	neuna
thinness	gÓnna	gÓnna	gÓnna	gÓnna	gÓnna	gÓnna
weakness	Ņ∂′ts∂′mna	taksapna	hatlou?na	hatlou?na	ta?sapna	ta?sapna
wisdom	či?na/pilna	pilna	pilna	pilna	pilna	pilna
love	ηai	ηai	ηai	ηai	ηai	ηai
long	sáu	sáu	sáu	sáu	sáu	sáu
good	p^{h}à	p^{h}à	p^{h}à	p^{h}à	p^{h}à	p^{h}à
wet	kÓt	čik	čé?	kÓt	kÓt	kÓt
mercy	lúηset	hepina	lúηset	he?pi?na	lúηsiatna	luηsia
obscure	∂muol	t^{h}íenglou	amoul	čiaηlou	čiaηlou	amual?
shining	va?/dol	va?/tesisel	va?	va?	va?	va?
straight	z∂′η	z∂′η	z∂′η	z∂′η	z∂′η	z∂′η
shame	zúm	zúm	zúm	zúm	zúm	zúm
wonder	l∂′md∂′η	l∂′md∂′η	l∂′md∂′η	l∂′md∂′η	l∂′md∂′η	l∂′md∂′η
soon	kin	kin	kin	kin	kin	kin
quick	g∂′η	g∂′η	g∂′η	g∂′η	g∂′η	g∂′η
beautiful	hÒi	hÒi	hÒi	hÒi	hÒi	hÒi
Adverbs of Direction and Measurement						
area of	∂letdan	∂letdan	∂letdan	∂letdan	∂letdan	∂letdan
bottom of	∂tÒlam	∂tÒlam	∂tÒlam	∂tÒlam	∂tÒlam	∂tÒlam
far	g∂′mŅa	g∂′mla	g∂′mla	g∂′mla	g∂′mla	g∂′mla
near	∂nai	∂nai	∂nai	∂nai	∂nai	∂nai

English	*Thadou*	*Vaiphei*	*Gangte*	*Paite*	*Simte*	*Zou*
northeast	sa?sÒl∂'m	malsua	malsuo?	malsua?	malsua	sa?sÒl∂'m
rectangle	níηlinei	níηlinei	níηlinei	killinei	níηlinei	níηlinei
half	∂kim	∂kim	∂kim(x∂'t)	∂kim(x∂'t)	∂kim(x∂'t)	∂kim(x∂'t)
south	siml∂'m	siml∂'m	siml∂'m	siml∂'m	siml∂'m	siml∂'m
upward	∂čuηl∂'m	∂čuηl∂'m	∂čuηl∂'m	∂tuηl∂'m	∂tuηl∂'m	∂tuηl∂'m
above	∂čuη	∂čuη	∂čuη	∂tuη	∂tuη	∂tuη
Adverbs of Time						
before	∂ma	∂mas∂'η	∂mas∂'η	∂ma	∂ma	∂ma
day after tomorrow	t^{h}aini	ziηkit	ziηkit	ziηhal	t^{h}aini	t^{h}aini
evening	niŊ̧∂'tl∂m	nit∂'kl∂m	nit∂'kl∂m	nit∂'kl∂m	nit∂'kl∂m	nit∂'kl∂m
full moonnight	Ŋ̧alitzàn	t^{h}ali?zàn	t^{h}alikzàn	xalikzàn	hali? zàn	haili? Zàn
night	zàn	zàn	zàn	zàn	zàn	zàn
sunset	niŊ̧úm	nisatúm	nisatúm	nitúm	nitúm	nitúm
yesterday	zàní	zàní	zàní	zàní	zàní	zàní
afternoon	sùnkìm	sùnkìm	sùnkìm	sunnúη	sùnnúη	sùnl∂'m
Functional Words						
above	∂čuηl∂m	∂čuηl∂m	∂čuηl∂m	∂tuηl∂m	∂tuηl∂m	∂tuηl∂m
against	∂dou	nialkàl	nielkàl	nielkàl?	nialkàl	niekàl
because	∂zi?	∂ziak	∂zekču?	∂ziak	∂zia?	∂zie?
except	tilou	tilou	ti?lou?	tellou in	čilou	čilou
if	ahiloule?	ahilou čun	ahi? le?	hilale?	ahile?	ahile?
sometimes	∂čáηčaη le?	∂čáηčaη le?	∂čáηčaη le?	∂táηtáηle?	∂táηtáηle?	∂táηtáηle?

English	*Thadou*	*Vaiphei*	*Gangte*	*Paite*	*Simte*	*Zou*
Numerals						
first	xatna	xatna	xatna	xatna	xatna	xatna
second	nina	nina	ni?na	ni?na	ni?na	nina
third	t^húmna	t^húmna	t^húmna	t^húmna	t^húmna	t^húmna
one	x∂`t	x∂`t	x∂`t	x∂`t	x∂`t	x∂`t
two	nì	nì	nì?	nì?	nì?	nì
three	t^húm	t^húm	t^húm	t^húm	t^húm	t^húm
four	lí	lí	lí?	lí	lí	lí
five	ηá	ηá	ηá?	ηá	ηá	ηá
six	gùp	gùk	gùp	gùk	gù?	gù?
seven	sagi	sagi	sagi?	sagi?	sagi	sagi
eight	giet	giat	giet	giat	giet	giet
nine	kó	kó	kó	kúa	kúa	kúo
ten	sÓm	sÓm	sÓm	sÓm	sÓm	sÓm
hundred	zà	zà	zà?	zà	zà	zà
thousand	sáη	sáη	sáη	síη	síη	síη
lakh	sáηza	nuaix∂`t	nuoi?	nuai	nuai	nuoi
million	nil	m∂`ktaduai	m∂`ktadoi	vaibelsia	m∂`ktaduai	m∂`?taduoi
crore	taimak	nuai zax∂`at	nuoizax∂`t	nuaizax∂`t	nuaizax∂`t	nuoizax∂`t
Verbs						
sell	zò?	zuak	zuak	zuak	zuak	zual
stitch	xùi	xùi	xùi	xùi	xùi	xùi
bury	vùi	vùi	vùi	vùi	vùi	vùi
cut into shape	sùi	sùi	sùi	sùi	sùi	sùi
keep	kÒi	kÒi	kÒi?	kÒi?	kÒi	kÒi
aim	dÒi	dÒi	dÒi	ηim	dÒi	dÒi

English	*Thadou*	*Vaiphei*	*Gangte*	*Paite*	*Simte*	*Zou*
lick	liek	liek	liak	liek	liek	liek
dance	làm	làm	làm	làm	làm	làm
weep	k∂`p	k∂`p	k∂`p	k∂`p	k∂`p	k∂`p
enter	lút	lút	lút	lút	lút	lút
see	mù	mù	mù	mù	mù	mù
give	pie	pie	pie	pie	pie	pie
feed	va?	vak	vak	vak	va?	va?
touch	tÒ?xa?	xÒi	suxa	xÒi?	xÒi?	t^{n}amxa?
insult	sù?zum	sù?zum	sùmolp^{n}óu	sùzum	musit	sù?zum
fine someone	g∂`p	g∂`p	g∂`p	g∂`p	g∂`p/liausa?	g∂`p
employ	gùi	gùi	gùi	gùi	gùi	gùi
mix	h∂`l	hel	hel	hel	h∂`l	kih∂`l
quit	hái	hái	hái	hái/top	hái/top	hái
appeal	ηe?na	dÒtna	ηe?na	ηen	ηe?na	ηetna
do	bÓl	bÓl	bÓl	bÓl	bÓl	bÓl
like something	dèi	dèi	dèi?	dèi?	dei/ut	dèi
speak	sei	gen	gen	gen	gen	gen
come	húη	húη	húη	húη	húη	húη
taste for food	dù	dù	dù	dù?	dù?	dù
defiled	subo?	subok	subuok	subuak	sut^{h}aη	subuo?
Miscellaneous						
name	min	min	min	min	min	min
thorn	liη	liη	liη	liη	liη	liη
smoke	xú	xú	xú	xú	xú	xú
near	∂nài	∂nài	∂nài	∂nài	∂nài	∂nài
fat	t^{h}áo	t^{h}áu	t^{h}áu	t^{h}áu	t^{h}áu	t^{h}áu
torn	∂sie	∂sie	∂sie	∂sie	∂sie	∂sie
short	nìem	nìem	nìem	nìem	nìem	nìem
path	l∂′mpi	l∂′mpi	l∂′mpi	l∂′mpi	l∂′mpi	l∂′mpi
money	súm	súm	súm	súm	súm	súm
ripe	∂mín	∂mín	∂mín	∂mín	∂mín	∂mín
dream	m∂′η	m∂′η	m∂′η	m∂′η	m∂′η	m∂′η

English	Thadou	Vaiphei	Gangte	Paite	Simte	Zou
mad	∂ηÓl	∂ηÓl	∂ηÓl	∂ηÓl	∂ηÓl	∂ηÓl
marriage	kičéη	kičéη	kičéη	kitéη	kitéη	kičéη
letter	lexat^{h}Ót	lexat^{h}Ót	lexat^{h}Ót	lait^{h}on	lexat^{h}Ót	lait^{h}Òt
sound	∂gin	∂gin	∂gin	∂giη	∂gin	∂gin
intellectual	čiη	pil	čiη	pil	pil	čiη
jeolousy	t^{h}∂'ηt^{h}ip	en	t^{h}∂'nt^{h}ip	en	eη	t^{h}∂'ηsia
lust	hu?	hu?	utča	huk	hù?	huo?
secret	t^{h}ugù?	t^{h}ugùk	gukt^{h}im	t^{h}ugùk	t^{h}ugù?	gu?sim
sorrow	Ņasetna	luηgim	luηxam	luηxam	luηxam	hasia?
suspicion	ginmÒ	giηmÒ	giηmÒ	giηmÒ	giηmÒ	giηmÒ
ignorant	∂mÓl	∂mÓl	∂mÓl	∂mÓl	∂mÓl	∂mÓl
success	lÒŅina	lÒtona	lÒtina	lÒ?činna	lÒ?činna	lÒčinna
friendship	loi/gólča	loi/gólča	loi/gólča	lÓm	lÓm	lÓm
tribute	zàna	zàna	zàna?	zà?na	zà?na	zàna
suddenly	kita?in	t^{h}axatnin	kita?in	t^{h}axatnin	t^{h}axata	t^{h}axatnin
mind	lúη	lúη	lúη	lúη	lúη	lúη
precious	m∂`ntam	m∂`ntam	m∂`ntam	m∂`np^{h}a	m∂`np^{h}a	m∂`ntam
bad smell	n∂`mse	n∂`mse	n∂`mse	n∂`mse	n∂`mse	n∂`mse
good smell	n∂`mtui	n∂`mtui	gimlim	n∂`mtui	n∂`mtui	n∂`mtui
sufficient	Ņiη	tiη	tiη	čiη	čiη	čiη
question marker	ná	mÓ	mÓ	mO	mO	mO
her	∂manu	∂manu	∂ma?nu	∂manu	∂manu	∂manu
I	kèi	kèi	kèi	kèi	kèi	kèi
you	n∂η	n∂η	n∂η	n∂η	n∂η	n∂η

APPENDIX-II

Word Correpondences Among the Kuki-Chin Languages

Correspondence between /č/ and /t/ in initial position:

English	*Thadou*	*Vaiphei*	*Gangte*	*Paite*	*Simte*	*Zou*
son/daughter	čá	čá	čá	tá	tá	tá
verses	čàŋ	čàŋ	čàŋ	tàŋ	tàŋ	tàŋ
equal part	čáŋ	čáŋ	čáŋ	táŋ	táŋ	táŋ
share	čàn	čàn	čàn	tàn	tàn	tàn
knife	čém	čém	čém	tém	tém	tém
lung	čúop	čúop	čúop	túop	túop	túop
live	čeŋ	čeŋ	čeŋ	teŋ	teŋ	teŋ
above	čúŋ	čúŋ	čúŋ	túŋ	túŋ	túŋ
bite	čú?	čú?	čú?	tú?	tú?	tú?
struggle to get	čù	čù	čù	tù	tù	tù
snail	tùilúŋ	čéŋkÓl	čéŋkÓl	téŋkÓl	téŋkÓl	téŋkÓl
bring	čói	čói	čói	tói	tói	tói
cover	čùn	čùn	čùn	tùn	tùn	tùn
compressed	čè	čè	čè	tè	tè	tè

Correspondence between /č/ and /t/ in medial position:

English	*Thadou*	*Vaiphei*	*Gangte*	*Paite*	*Simte*	*Zou*
marriage	kičéŋ	kičéŋ	kičéŋ	kitéŋ	kitéŋ	kitéŋ
shifting	kičÓ́n	kičÓ́n	kičÓ́n	kitÓ́n	kitÓ́n	kitÓ́n
bounce	kičÓn	kičÓn	kičÓn	kičÓn	kičÓn	kičÓn

English	Thadou	Vaiphei	Gangte	Paite	Simte	Zou
kiss	kičòp	kičòp	kičòp	kitòp	kitòp	kitòp
alter	maičam	maičam	maičam	maitam	maitam	maitam
earth's surface	leičúŋ	leičúŋ	leičúŋ	letčúŋ	letčúŋ	letčúŋ
thirsty	də̂ŋčáʔ	dƏŋčáʔ	də̂ŋčáʔ	dƏŋtáʔ	də̂ŋtáʔ	də̂ŋtáʔ
chilly	mə̂lča	mƏlča	mƏlča	mƏlča	mə̂lča	mə̂lča
surgarcane	kÓlčú	kÓlčú	kÓlčú	kÓ!tú	kÓltú	kÓltú
heart	luŋčə̂ŋ	luŋčə̂ŋ	luŋčə̂ŋ	luŋtƏŋ	luŋtə̂ŋ	luŋtə̂ŋ
stubborn	loučə̂l	loučə̂l	loučə̂l	loutə̂l	loučə̂l	loutə̂t
ox	boŋčə̂l	boŋčə̂l	boŋčə̂l	boŋtə̂l	boŋtə̂l	boŋtə̂l
woodpecker	ŋeičál	ŋeičál	neičál	ŋeitál	ŋeitál	ŋeitál
scissor	bàʔče	bàʔče	bàʔče	bàʔtče	bàʔtče	bàʔtče

Correspondence between /č/ and /p/ in initial position:

English	Thadou	Vaiphei	Gangte	Paite	Simte	Zou
clever	číŋ	číŋ	číŋ	píl	píl	píl
go	čì	čì	čì	péi	péi	péi

Correspondence Between /č/ and /l/ in Initial Position:

English	Thadou	Vaiphei	Gangte	Paite	Simte	Zou
peace	čƏmna	čƏmna	čƏmna	liemna	liemna	liemna
buy	čÓʔ	čÓʔ	čÓʔ	léi	léi	léi

Correspondence Between /Ŋ̦/, /t^h/, and /h/ in Initial Position:

English	*Thadou*	*Vaiphei*	*Gangte*	*Paite*	*Simte*	*Zou*
moon	Ŋ̦a	t^ha	t^ha	k^ha	ha	ha
spirit	Ŋ̦agao	t^hagao	t^hagao	k^hagau	hagau	hagau
sweet	Ŋ̦um	t^hum	t^hum	k^hum	hum	hum
wing	Ŋ̦a	t^ha	t^ha	k^ha	ha	ha
area of hill	Ŋ̦aŋ	t^haŋ	t^haŋ	k^haŋ	k^haŋ	k^haŋ
duplicate	Ŋ̦em	t^hem	t^hem	k^hem	k^hem	k^hem

Correspondence Between /Ŋ̦/ and /t/ in Initial Position:

English	*Thadou*	*Vaiphei*	*Gangte*	*Paite*	*Simte*	*Zou*
run	Ŋ̦Ŋ̦ei	tai	tai	tai	tai	tai
setting of the sun	Ŋ̦Ŋ̦ùm	tùm	tùm	tùm	tùm	tùm
weak	Ŋ̦tasƏm	tasƏm	tasƏm	tasƏm	tasƏm	tasƏm

Correspondence Between /Ŋ̦/, /t/ and /č/ in Initial Position:

English	*Thadou*	*Vaiphei*	*Gangte*	*Paite*	*Simte*	*Zou*
sufficient	Ŋ̦ing	tiŋ	tiŋ	čiŋ	čiŋ	čiŋ
block	tíŋ	tíŋ	tíŋ	číŋ	číŋ	číŋ

Correspondence Between /t^h/ and /s/ in Initial Position:

English	*Thadou*	*Vaiphei*	*Gangte*	*Paite*	*Simte*	*Zou*
ginger	t^hiŋ	t^hiŋ	t^hiŋ	siŋ	siŋ	siŋ
wood	t^hiŋ	t^hiŋ	t^hiŋ	siŋ	siŋ	siŋ
Iron	t^hi?	t^hik	t^hik	sik	sik	sik
blood	t^hisən	t^hisən	t^hisən	sisən	sisən	sisən
die	t^hi	t^hi	t^hi	si	si	si
liver	t^hin	t^hin	t^hin	si	si	si
quite	t^hip	t^hip	t^hip	sip	sip	sip
ghost	t^hiN̦a	t^hitha	t^hitha	sikha	sikha	sikha
branch	t^hiŋbaʔ	t^hiŋbaʔ	t^hiŋbaʔ	siŋbaʔ	siŋbaʔ	siŋbaʔ
box	t^hiŋbom	t^hiŋbom	t^hiŋbom	siŋbom	siŋbom	siŋbom

Bibliography

Abbi, Anvita, 1990, Reduplication in Tibeto-Burman. *South Asian Studies*, 28.2:171-181, Fall 1990.

Abbi, Anvita, 1992. *Reduplication in South Asian Languages: An Areal, Typological and Historical Study,* Allied Publishers Limited, New Delhi.

Abbi, Anvita, 1997, *Languages of Tribal and Indigenous Peoples of India,* Motilal Banarsidass Publishers Private Limited, Delhi.

Abraham, P.T., 1985, *Apatani Grammar,* CIIL, Mysore.

Acharya, K.P., 1983, *Lotha Grammar,* CIIL, Mysore.

Amickal, Joseph, 1992, *Maram Naga: A Socio-Cultural Study,* Mittal Publications, New Delhi-110059.

Arokianathan, S., 1980, *Tangkhul Naga Phonetic Reader,* CIIL, Mysore.

Bampbell, George, 1875, *Specimens of The Languages of India, Including Those of the Aboriginal Tribes of Bengal, The Central Provinces and Eastern Frontiers*, Bengal: Secretariat Press, Calcutta, Bengal.

Baruah, P.N.D., *Hmar Grammar,* CIIL, Mysore.

Beckwith, Christopher 1, 2003, *Medial Tibeto-Burman Languages*, Brill Academic Publishers, Leiden.

Benedict, Paul K., 1973, Tibeto-Burman Tones, With a Note on Teleo-Reconstruction, *Ao* 35: 127-38.

Benedict, Paul. K, 1948, *Tonal Systems in Southeast Asia. JAOS*, 68:184-91.

Bhat, D.N.S., 1844, *The Adjectival Category: Criteria for Differentiation and Identification.* John Benjamins Pub.Co.

Bhat, D.N.S., 1988, *Grammatical Relations in Indian Languages (An Introduction to Indian Grammar 1)*, CIIL, Mysore.

Bhat, D.N.S., 1991. *Grammatical Relations: The Evidence Against their Necessity and Universality*. Routledge, London.

Bradley, David, 1997, Tibeto-Burman Languages and Classification, The Tibeto-Burman Languages of the Himalayas, paper in *SEALS* 14:1-72, Pacific Linguistics A-56, Australian National University, Canberra.

Bradley, David, 2002, *The subgrouping of the Tibeto-Burman, Medieval Tibeto-Burman Languages*, ed. by Christopher, Beckwith, pp. 73-112, Brill Academic Publishers, Leiden.

Bright, William, 1960, *Linguistic Change in Some Caste Dialects, Linguistic Diversity in South Asia*, ed., by Charles A. Ferguson and J. Gumperrz., pp. 19-26, Indiana University Research Centre in Anthropology, Folklore and Linguistics, Bloomington.

Buchanan, Francis, 1998, A Comparative Vocabulary of Some of the Languages Spoken in Burma Empire, AR 5: 219-40.

Burling, Robbins, 2003, "*The* Tibeto-Burman Languages of the North-Eastern India" in Graham Thurgood and Randy J. LaPolla, eds. *The Sino-Tibetan Languages.* London and New York: Routledge.

Burling, Robbins, 2007, Language, Ethnicity and Migration in North-Eastern India, *Journal of South Asian Studies* 30:3, pp. 391-404.

Burling, Robins, 1961, *A Garo Grammar*, Deccan College Postgraduate and Research Institute.

Carey, Bertram S., and H.N. Tuck, 1987, *The Chin Hills,* Gian Publishing House, Delhi.

Census of India, (2001), New Delhi: Registrar General and Census Commissioner, India.

Census of India, Manipur State (2001), New Delhi: Registrar General and Census Commissioner, India.

Chaklader, Snehamoy, 1990, *A Sociolinguistics: A Guide to Language Problems in India.* Mittal Publications, New Delhi.

DeLancey, Scott, 1987, "Sino-Tibetan Languages" in Berrnard Comrie, ed., *The World's Major Languages,* New York. Oxford University Press.

Driem Van, George, 2007 c, "Endangered Languages of South Asia", pp. 303-341 in Matthias Brenzinger, ed. *Handbook of Endangered Languages.* Berlin: Mouton de Gruyter.

Driem Van, George, 2007, "The Diversity of the Tibeto-Burman Language Family and Linguistic Ancestry of Chinese", Bulletin of Chinese Linguistics, 1 (2): 211-270.

Dua, Hans R., 1986, *Language Use, Attitudes and Identity Among Linguistic Minorities (A Case Study of Dakkhini Urdu Speakers in Mysore),* CIIL, Mysore.

Dua, Hans R., 1992, *Communication Policy and Language Planning,* Yashoda Publications, Mysore.

Elangaiyan, R., "Strategies Propose for Arresting Language Endangerment in India," in Elangaiyan, R., R. Brown, *et al.*, eds., 2006, *Proceedings of the* FEL-X, CIIL, Mysore and FELX UK.

Enfield, N.J., *Areal Linguistics and Mainland Southeast Asia*, Language and Cognition Group, Max Planck Institute for Psycholinguistics, PB 310, 6500 AH, Nijmega, The Netherlands.

Fasold, Ralph, 1984, *Sociolinguistic of Society, Introduction to Sociolinguistics Vol.,* Blackwell Publishers.

Giglioli, Pier Paolo, ed, 1972, *Language and Social Context,* Penguin Books Ltd., Harmondsworth, Middlesex, England.

Giridhar, P.P., 1980, *Angami Grammar,* CIIL, Mysore.

Gordon, Raymond G., Jr. (ed.), 2005, *Ethnologue: Languages of the World,*

Fifteenth edition, Dallas, Tex.: SIL International. Online version, http://www.ethnologue.com/.

Gowda, K. S. Gurubasave, 1975, *Ao Grammar,* CIIL, Mysore, 1975.

Grierson, G. A., 1903, *Linguistic Survey of India, Vol. III, Part II,* Calcutta: Government Printing.

Grierson, G. A., 1909, *Linguistic Survey of India, Vol. III, Part I,* Calcutta: Government Printing.

Grierson, G. A., 1904, *Linguistic Survey of India, Vol. III, Part III,* Calcutta: Government Printing.

Haokip, Pauthang, January 2008, "Phonological Structure of Thadou," *South Asian Language Review*, Vol.XVIII.1.

Haokip, Pauthang, November 2009, "Noun Morphology in Kuki-Chin Language," *Language in India*, Vol. 9:11.

Hasnain, Imtiaz, S.,(ed), 1995, *Standardization and Modernization: Dynamics of Language Planning,* Bahri Publications, New Delhi.

Hatzaw, H.S., 2003, *Christianity in Manipur,* Published by Hang Za Kam, Churachandpur, Manipur, India.

Henderson, Eugenie, J.A., 1948, Notes on the Syllable Structure of Lushai, *BS0AS*12:713-725.

Hodson, T.C., 2007 (1911), *The Naga Tribes of Manipur*, Low Price Publication, Delhi.

Hodson, Thomas Callan, 1906, *Thado Grammar,* Shillong.

Houghton, Bernard, 1896, *Outlines of a Tibeto-Burman Linguistics Paleontology, JRAS* 23-55.

Houghton, Bernhard, 1892, *Essay on the Languages of Southern Chin and its Affinities,* Rangoon: Government Printing Office.

Jacquesson, Francois, 2001, Person-Marking in Tibeto-Burman Languages, North-Eastern India, Person and Evidence in the *Himalayan Languages*, ed. by Balthasar Bickel, 2000, *Special Issue of LTBA* Vol II:24.1:113-144.

Jeyapaul, V.Y., 1987, *Karbi Grammar,* CIIL, Mysore.

Jha, Lambodar, 1989, *Kinship Terms in the Languages of Manipur*, Paper Presented at the 2nd National Seminar on Tibeto-Burman Linguistics, Manipur University, Imphal.

Joesph, U.V., and Burling, R., 2006, *The Comparative Phonology of the Boro Garo Languages,* CIIL, Mysore.

Joseph, U.V., and Burling, Robbins, 2006, *The Comparative Phonology of the Boro Garo Languages,* CIIL, Mysore.

Kabui, Gangmumei,1995, "Genesis of the Naga and the Kukis," in Sanajaoba Naorem, (ed.) *Manipur Past and Present,* Vol. 3. Mittal Publications, New Delhi.

Kapfo, Kedutso, 2005, *The Ethnology of the Khezhas and the Khezha Grammar,* CIIL, Mysore.

Karapurkar, P. P., 1976, *Kokborok Grammar*, CIIL, Mysore.

Lebar, Frank M., Gerald C., Hickey, and John K., Musgrave, 1964, *Ethnic Groups of Mainland Southeast Asia*, Human Relations Area Files, INC, New Heaven.

Lee Cooper, Robert, 1984, *Language Planning and Social Change,* Cambridge University Press. Cambridge. New York Portchester Melbourne Sydney.

Lehman, F.K., 1975c, Wolfenden's Non-Pronominal A-Prefix in Tibeto-Burman: two Arguments from Southern Chin and some Proposed Semantic Correlates, *LTBA* 2.1:19-44.

Lehman, F.K., 1990, Outline of A Formal Syntax of Numerical Expression with Special Reference to the Phenomenon of Numerical Classifiers, *LTBA* 13.1:89-120.

Lewin, Thomas Herbert, 2004, *Wild Races of the Eastern Frontier of India*, Mittal [reported from 1870: London], New Delhi.

Lieut. Col. Surg. Reid. M.B. A.S. 1976 (1893), *Chin-Lushei Land including A Description of the various Expeditions into The Chin-Lushei Hills and the Final Annexation of the Country,* Firma-Kim Private Ltd. on behalf of Tribal Research Institute, Aizawl, Mizoram.

Maddieson, Ian, 1977, *Universal Tone: Six Studies*, University of California Ph.D. Thesis, Los Angeles.

Maddieson, Ian, 2002, *Typological Patterns of Phonological Systems in Geographical Perspective,* Paper presented at the 17th Annual Meeting of the Linguistic Society of America, January 3-6, 2002.

Makenzie, Alexander, 1884, *History of the Relations of the Government with the Hill Tribes of Northeast Frontier of Bengal*, Home Department Press, Calcutta.

Matisoff, James A., 2003, *Handbook of Proto-Tibetan-Burman: System and Philosophy of Sino-Tibetan Reconstruction,* University of California Press, Berkeley and Los Angeles, California.

McCulloch, Major W., 1859, *Account of the Valley of Munnipore and the Hill Tribes, with a Comparative Vocabulary of Munnipore and their Languages.* Calcutta: Bengal Printing Co.

Mittal, K.M., ed, 1988, *The Paite:, A Transborder Tribe of India and Burman*, Mittal Publications, Delhi.

Mortensen, David, 2003, *Comparative Tangkhul,* University of California, Berkeley. (posted on internet)

Nag, Chitta Ranjan, 1993, *The Mizo Society in Transition*, Vikas Publishing House, New Delhi.

Needham, Rodney, 1959, "Vaiphei Social Structure", *AmAn* 62:236-53, and *SJA* 15.4: 390-406, Winter 1959.

Needham, Rodney, 1960, "A Structural Analysis of Aimol Society", *BTLV* 116:81-108.

Needham, Rodney, 1960, "Chawte Social Structure", *AmAn* 62:235-53.

Nunthora, C., 1996, *Mizoram: Society and Polity,* Indus Publishing Co., Mizoram.

Ostler, Nicholas, (ed), 1999, *Endangered Languages: What Role for the Specialists?* in Proceedings of the Second FEL Conference held at the Pollock Halls, University of Edinburgh, 25-27 September 1998.

Pakem, B., 1990, *Nationality, Ethnicity and Cultural Identity in Northeast India*, Omsons Publications, New Delhi.

Position Paper 1.3: National Focus Group on Teaching of Indian Languages, November 2006, NCERT, New Delhi.

Prasad, Bal Ram, 1991, *Mishing Grammar,* CIIL Press, Mysore.

Ramaswami, N., 1999, *Common Linguistic Features in Indian Languages: Phonetics,* CIIL, Mysore.

Reid, Sir Robert, 1997 (1942), *History of the Frontier Areas Bordering on Assam from 1883-1941*, Spectrum Publications, Guwahati: Delhi.

Sastry, G.D.P., 1984, *Mishmi Phonetic Reader,* CIIL, Mysore.

Shafer, R., 1966, *Introduction to Sino-Tibetan,* Wiesbaden: Otto Harrassowitz.

Shakespear, Lt. Colonel, J., 1975 (1912), *The Lushei Kuki Clans,* Tribal Research Institute, Aizawl, Mizoram.

Shaw, William, 1983, *The Thadou Kukis (1929),* Cultural Publishing House, Delhi.

Singh, Chungkham Jashwanta, 1995, *The Linguistic Situation in Manipur,* Linguistics of the Tibeto-Burman Area, Vol. 18:1-Spring.

Singh, Chungkham Yashwanta, 2000, *Manipuri Grammar,* Rajesh Publications, New Delhi.

Singh, Inder, 1975, *Manipuri Phonetic Reader,* CIIL, Mysore.

Singh, K.S. (eds), 1998, *People of India, Manipur, Vol.XXXI,* Anthropological Survey of India, Calcutta.

Singh, Naorem Saratchandra, 2006, *A Grammar of Paite,* Mittal Publication, Delhi.

Singson, T.S. Agou, 2001, *Thadou Kuki Suongmantam Dictionary.*

Sreedhar, M.V., 1980, *Sema Grammar,* CIIL, Mysore.

Stewart, Lt. R., 1857, "Slight notice of the Grammar of Thadou or New Kookies Language", *Journal of Asia Society of Bengal.*

Tensuba, K.C., 1993, *An Approach to the History of Meiteis and Thais*, New Delhi Inter-India.

Than, Tin, 1928, "A Short Account of Taungthas", *JBRS* 18:16-20, Rangoon.

Thanga, L.B., 1978, *The Mizos: A Study in Racial Personality*, United Publication, Guwahati.

Thirumalai, M.S., 1972, *Thaadou Phonetic Reader,* CIIL, Mysore.

Thirumalai, M.S., 2004, "Thadou Linguistic Situation in Manipur," *Language in India, Vol. 4.*

Trudgill, Peter, 1974, *Sociolinguistics: An Introduction to Language and Society,* Penguin Books Ltd., Harmondsworth, Middlesex, England.

Vaiphei, Kim, 1995, *The Coming of Christianity in Manipur, With Special Reference to the Kukis*, Joint Women's Programme, New Delhi.

VanBik, Kenneth, N.D., In search of the origin of the names Kuki-Chin, Berkeley: University of California, Department of Linguistics, http:www.chro.org/index.php/scholar section/144.

Vumson and *Zo History: With An Introduction to Zo Culture, Economy, Religion and their Status as an Ethnic Minority in India, Burma and Bangladesh,* Venglhlui, Aizawl, Mizoram.

Win, Tin Win, and Maung Aung Bwint, 1995, *Travels on Chin Hills: A Comprehensive Description of Present Days Life in Chin State, Burma*, Videosoft Production, Rangoon.

Woodthorpe, R.G., *Lushai Expedition*, Hurst and Blackett.

Wright, Sue, 2004, *Language Policy and Language Planning from Nationalism to Globalisation,* Palgrave Macmillan, New York.

Index